QUICK AND EASY PASTA RECIPES

REVISED

Coleen and Bob Simmons

BRISTOL PUBLISHING ENTERPRISES, INC.
San Leandro, California

A Nitty Gritty® Cookbook

Printed in the United States of America.

ISBN 1-55867-050-5

Cover design: Frank Paredes
Cover photography: John Benson
Food stylist: Suzanne Carreiro
Illustrator: Joan Baakkonen

CONTENTS

SERVE CREATIVE, EASY, NUTRITIOUS MEALS WITH NITTY GRITTY® COOKBOOKS

Cooking with Parchment Paper
The Garlic Cookbook
Flatbreads From Around the World
From Your Ice Cream Maker
Favorite Cookie Recipes revised
Cappuccino/Espresso: The Book of
  Beverages
Indoor Grilling
Slow Cooking
The Best Pizza is Made at Home
The Well Dressed Potato
Convection Oven Cookery
The Steamer Cookbook
The Pasta Machine Cookbook
The Versatile Rice Cooker
The Dehydrator Cookbook
The Bread Machine Cookbook
The Bread Machine Cookbook II
The Bread Machine Cookbook III

The Bread Machine Cookbook IV
The Bread Machine Cookbook V
Worldwide Sourdoughs From Your
  Bread Machine
Recipes for the Pressure Cooker
The New Blender Book
The Sandwich Maker Cookbook
Waffles
The Coffee Book
The Juicer Book
The Juicer Book II
Bread Baking (traditional), revised
The Kid's Cookbook
No Salt, No Sugar, No Fat
  Cookbook, revised
Cooking for 1 or 2, revised
Quick and Easy Pasta Recipes,
  revised
15-Minute Meals for 1 or 2

The 9x13 Pan Cookbook
Extra-Special Crockery Pot Recipes
Chocolate Cherry Tortes and
  Other Lowfat Delights
Low Fat American Favorites
Now That's Italian!
Fabulous Fiber Cookery
Low Salt, Low Sugar, Low Fat
  Desserts
Healthy Cooking on the Run,
  revised
Healthy Snacks for Kids
Muffins, Nut Breads and More
The Wok
New Ways to Enjoy Chicken
Favorite Seafood Recipes
New International Fondue Cookbook
Authentic Mexican Cooking

Write or call for our free catalog.
BRISTOL PUBLISHING ENTERPRISES, INC.
P.O. Box 1737, San Leandro, CA 94577
(800) 346-4889; in California (510) 895-4461

INTRODUCTION

Enjoy pasta often with a clear conscience — it's good for you! Pasta is one of America's favorite dishes because it is a satisfying, wholesome food, not high in calories. It can be prepared quickly and in many different ways and combined with a wide variety of other healthful foods. A satisfying portion of pasta (about two ounces of dried pasta or three ounces of fresh pasta before cooking) has slightly more than 200 calories before the addition of a sauce or seasoning. The seasonings can be very pungent because the taste moderates when mixed with the blandness of pasta. Assertive ingredients such as garlic, strong cheese, anchovies and hot peppers can be used in small amounts to give pasta a delicious flavor without adding large number of calories.

In the pages that follow, you'll find information about ingredients, directions for making homemade pasta, and recipes for pasta using fresh seasonal vegetables. Fast, delicious sauces, new salad combinations, pasta with meats and new twists on baked pasta dishes will tempt you. If you are like we are, you will never tire of pasta — it's eating at its best.

THE RIGHT INGREDIENTS

ABOUT DRIED PASTA

All dried pastas are of similar composition. They contain hard durum wheat, sometimes with the addition of egg and possibly flavoring or coloring ingredients. There is a wide variation in the "bite" in pastas, even between those made only of wheat and water. The very best pastas tend to be those imported from Italy, with some brands being vastly superior to others. The brands available vary from region to region, so the best approach is to try two or three of the Italian pastas and decide which is best. Two of our favorites brands are Delverde and DaVinci. A high quality pasta will keep its pale yellow color during cooking, and the cooking water will not become cloudy. Start with one shape, such as linguine, and try it with a simple sauce that really lets the wheaty flavor of the pasta shine through. When you find a brand that pleases you, stick with it and try the various shapes.

There are myriad shapes, colors, and flavors of dried pastas from which to choose. The new dried lasagne noodles no longer have to be precooked — just layer with sauce and cheese, and then microwave or bake to perfection. There are specialty pastas made of grains other than wheat for people on restricted diets.

ABOUT FRESH PASTA

Supermarket and deli cases today carry spectacular arrays of fresh pasta shapes and ready-to-heat-and-eat sauces. Fresh lasagne noodles are sold by the pound, ready to layer with cheese and sauce, and then be baked. Tortellini and agnolotti are filled with tasty stuffings. Tomato sauces come thin, thick, or chunky. Some of these products are very good, others mediocre. Excellent fresh pasta can be made at home; we have included instructions and recipes for making your own.

You will find you prefer certain pasta shapes with specific sauces. Light, delicate sauces tend to go better with thinner pastas. Hearty full-flavored sauces need more substantial pastas. Generally, dried pasta is best for making salads and serving with uncooked sauces because it has more "bite." Fresh egg pastas become soft and mushy in a salad preparations, but are wonderful with any sauce based on butter and cream.

Extra virgin olive oils, olive pastes, sun-dried tomatoes packed dry or in oil, and fresh herbs make quick pasta flavorings. Pesto, garlic puree, anchovy paste and sun-dried tomato paste are available in squeeze tubes when you need a tablespoon or two, and keep well in the refrigerator.

ABOUT OLIVE OILS

Wonderful olive oils come from Italy, Spain, France, Greece, and California. They range in color from pale yellow to deep green. Oils from Tuscany are light and elegant; Greek, Spanish and Sicilian olive oils tend to be more robust and full-flavored, and deeper green in color. Californian olive oils are also quite green in color. The soil and climate, of course, give the olive oils their unique characters. Look for oils that are clear and smell like olives. Olive oil has a limited shelf life after opening, so buy small bottles of several different brands until you find the ones you prefer. You definitely want to have at least one extra virgin olive oil and one or two full-flavored virgin or pure olive oils on hand. Store olive oil in a cool, dark place, but not in the refrigerator.

Extra virgin oils are hand pressed oils and generally are not used for heavy frying because they lose fragrance and charm when heated, and tend to burn more easily.

Make your own garlic-flavored olive oil to give a little extra tang to your simple pasta sauces or for making a quick toasted garlic bread. Heat ½ cup light olive oil, ⅛ tsp. red pepper flakes and 6 to 8 garlic cloves, peeled and smashed, in a small heavy saucepan over very low heat for about 15 minutes, or until garlic is very lightly browned. Remove from heat and let garlic cool in oil. Strain and place in a small airtight jar for storage.

ABOUT TOMATOES

The preferred fresh tomato for use in pasta sauces is the Romano or Italian. It is slightly oval, about the size of a large egg, and has very few seeds. The next best tomato is the perfectly ripe salad tomato which has been peeled and seeded. If ripe, full-flavored tomatoes are not available, buy a good brand of canned Italian plum tomatoes, preferably packed in rich tomato juice. Canned ready-cut peeled tomatoes in juice are available plain, or with Italian or Mexican herbs.

Unless you have a great surplus of tomatoes there is no reason to start with fresh tomatoes for sauces that require long simmering. The end result is little different from that made with canned tomato sauce or tomato paste.

If you are using canned tomatoes, hold the tomato over a sieve which has been set in a small bowl. With a small knife cut out the hard stem end and discard. Cut tomatoes in half lengthwise, and gently squeeze to remove most of the seeds. After all the tomatoes have been seeded, pour the juice remaining in the can through the sieve. If the recipe does not call for the tomato juice, reserve if for another purpose. Chop the tomatoes and add to the sauce you are making at the last minute to preserve their best color and texture.

ABOUT PEPPERS

The distinctive taste of peppers, whether they are green or yellow, mild or hot, fresh or dried, cooked or raw, complements the bland taste and smooth texture of pasta very well. The Italians often add a few red pepper flakes to a simmering sauce, or sprinkle a few flakes over a completed dish. Your taste will have to determine the amount used. People who love spicy food can eat and enjoy dishes that would make others turn red and go running for the water faucet.

Many recipes call for red or green bell peppers. These can be used without peeling, but most recipes will be greatly improved if the peppers are peeled. The very best way to peel a pepper is to cut the pepper into quarters along the natural depressions and peel it with a sharp vegetable peeler. Then remove the seeds and ribs, and cut the pepper into desired shapes. Peeled peppers cook more rapidly, stay crisper and tend to be easier on sensitive digestive systems.

Roasting peppers to peel them produces a basically cooked pepper. Start by placing the pepper under the broiler or over a barbecue fire or gas flame, turning frequently to char all sides. When the skin is blistered, place under a bowl or in a plastic bag to steam for about 15 minutes. The skin will soften and will pull off easily. Cut the peeled pepper into the desired shape. Roasted peppers can be stored in the refrigerator from 2 to 3 days if covered with water with a little vinegar added, or they can be frozen for future use.

ABOUT CHEESES

The very best hard cheese to grate over pasta is aged Italian Parmigiano-Reggiano. It is dry but not grainy and the flavor is assertive, but not sharp. Not only does it taste better, but it is also more economical to buy Parmigiano by the piece at a good Italian delicatessen or specialty cheese shop and grate it fresh as needed. A chunk of ungrated cheese, well wrapped, can be keep for months in the freezer or several weeks in the refrigerator. Beware of "imported Parmesan," "imported Italian," and "Italian-type" cheeses, especially if sold grated, because these will invariably be inferior to the real Parmigiano.

The other Italian cheese often used with pasta is Romano, which is made from sheep's milk. It has a much more assertive flavor than Parmigiano and tends to be more salty. It is better used in sauces and stuffing than as a grating cheese.

There are other cheeses well enough aged to be properly dry and mellow for grating over pasta. Aged provolone, Gouda, Monterey Jack, asiago, sapsago, and goat cheese all work well when grated fresh over pasta. Some markets now feature different kinds of grated cheese in convenient small containers. The grated cheese sold in shaker-top cans in supermarkets may be adequate for use in sauces, but should only be used as a last resort for other purposes.

Feta, mascarpone, and fresh goat cheeses are excellent for tossing with hot pasta, and make a quick creamy sauce.

MAKING YOUR OWN PASTA

The best pasta you will ever eat is that which you make fresh at home. Salt, oil and egg content can be controlled according to the tastes and dietary needs of the people who will eat it. It does take time and energy, but the results are delicious and very satisfying.

ABOUT FLOURS

If it is available, unbleached bread flour makes a firmer pasta with more of a "bite" like the Italian pastas, but all-purpose flour can be used for all of these recipes. Semolina or hard wheat durum flours can be substituted for at least part of the flour in most recipes. The best semolina flour is finely ground and should be specifically labeled as being for pasta. Pasta made with semolina flour will require extra liquid, and needs to rest longer before being rolled out. We don't recommend making semolina dough unless you have a pasta machine.

ABOUT EGGS

Always use the freshest eggs available. The eggs used in the recipes in this book are Grade A large. If using other than large eggs, mix the yolks and whites gently and use three tablespoons of the mixture for each egg called for in the recipe. Eggs at room temperature blend the best with flour.

BASIC HOMEMADE PASTA

This recipe makes slightly over a pound of delicious pasta.

2 cups bread flour
½ tsp. salt
3 large eggs at room temperature
2 tbs. olive oil
1-2 tbs. water if needed

MIXING PASTA DOUGH

Mixing pasta by hand: Combine flour and salt. Place in a dome on the counter or mixing surface. Make a well in the flour. Break eggs into the well, add olive oil, and with a kitchen fork gently beat the eggs and stir a little of the flour from the edges into eggs. Continue stirring until eggs and flour are combined and mixture is too stiff to continue stirring with a fork. Gently knead in remaining flour the same way you would knead bread dough, pushing, folding and turning for about 10 minutes, or until the dough is smooth and elastic.

You will find that handmade pasta dough is more difficult to knead than bread dough. Wrap the dough in plastic wrap and let it rest at room temperature for at least 15 to 20 minutes, or longer, before rolling and cutting.

Mixing pasta with a heavy duty mixer: Use any of the pasta recipes in this book. Place all ingredients in mixing bowl and beat with paddle or kneading hook until dough forms a ball and cleans the sides of the mixing bowl. Turn out of bowl and if dough is sticky, knead in a little flour. Wrap dough in plastic wrap and allow to rest for 20 minutes or longer before rolling and cutting.

Mixing pasta in a food processor: The food processor makes easy work of mixing a one-pound recipe of pasta dough. With the metal blade in place, combine the flour and salt in food processor bowl and pulse a few times to mix well. Break eggs into measuring cup, add olive oil and other liquid ingredients; pour through the feed tube while the processor is running. If everything is perfect, in about 15 to 20 seconds all the ingredients will be mixed and the sides of the bowl will be clean. The pasta will have the texture of coarse meal, but will hold together when pinched between the thumb and forefinger. It should not stick to the fingers. If the pasta is dry or not completely mixed, add a teaspoonful of water, process for a few seconds more, and check again. If the pasta dough is sticky, add more flour a tablespoon at a time until the proper consistency is reached. Remove the dough from the bowl, and gather into a ball.

Because the food processor has already partially kneaded the dough you will only have to knead it a minute until smooth. Wrap dough in plastic wrap. Allow it to rest for 20 minutes or longer before rolling out.

ROLLING PASTA DOUGH

Rolling by hand: Divide the rested dough into quarters. Dust a heavy rolling pin with flour. On a lightly floured surface roll out one piece of dough at a time into a large thin rectangular shape about 1/16-inch thick. Do not roll dough for more than 10 minutes, or it may become dry and lose its elasticity. Keep the remaining dough covered with a damp paper towel to prevent it from drying out. Repeat the rolling with the remaining pieces of dough. Place rolled pasta pieces on a clean towel and allow to rest for a few minutes until they feel dry to the touch and look slightly leathery. The pasta is now ready to cut. Drying the dough before cutting will help prevent the cut noodles from sticking together.

Rolling with a roller-type machine: There are two kinds of roller machines: hand-cranked and electric. Both knead and roll the pasta dough in the same way. The advantage of the electric machine is that you have two free hands for handling the dough.

After the pasta dough has been mixed either by hand, with a heavy duty mixer, or with a food processor as directed above, let it rest 15 to 20 minutes. Then divide the dough into two or three pieces and knead with the machine instead of by hand. Set the pasta machine rollers at the widest setting and run the dough through the machine until it becomes smooth and pliable. Fold the dough into thirds lengthwise after each pass, and run through the machine again. When the dough is pliable and very smooth, set the rollers to the next narrowest setting, fold the dough in half and run through the rollers two times. Set the rollers to the next narrowest setting and repeat rolling and narrowing until the desired thickness is reached. If using the electric roller machine, use the narrowest setting only if you are making won ton squares or filo dough, as this setting produces an extremely thin dough.

CUTTING PASTA DOUGH

Cutting by hand: Roll the dry, but still pliable dough loosely into a flat roll about 3 inches wide. Cut the pasta with a very sharp knife into desired widths. Press down firmly and cut, keeping the slices as even as possible. Don't saw. As soon as the whole roll has been cut, unroll so the noodles can dry further. Fettuccine is cut about 1/4-inch wide; noodles can range from 3/8-inch to 1 inch; lasagne can be cut into squares, or wide or narrow strips; manicotti and cannelloni wrappers are made by cutting pasta in 3-inch or 4-inch squares. The squares are cooked and then wrapped around a filling to form a cylinder.

Cutting pasta with a hand-cranked roller machine: Allow the rolled pasta dough to dry 15 to 20 minutes before cutting. Fit the machine with the desired cutting attachment. Before running dough through cutting rollers, cut sheets of pasta into strips that fit the machine and are the length you want the finished pasta to be. Lightly flour dough if it is at all sticky, and run through the cutter roller.

It is important that you *never* wash your roller machine. It should be carefully cleaned with a soft brush. The dried particles will fall out easily.

Cutting pasta with an electric roller machine: This machines operates exactly as the hand-cranked machine. Follow the same directions. The advantage is that you have two free hands for handling the strips of pasta. It also gets the job done in a hurry. *Never* wash this machine. Brush the dried particles out with a soft brush.

Your pasta is now ready to cook, or it can be stored in the refrigerator well-wrapped for a few days before being cooked; or it can be dried thoroughly and stored in an airtight container.

DRYING PASTA

If you've just made a batch of delicious pasta, you're probably going to want to eat it as soon as possible. However, it can be made ahead of time and allowed to dry. Once pasta is thoroughly dry, it can be stored in an airtight container just as though it were a commercial product. To dry, take strands of pasta and loop them around your fingers. Let dry on a kitchen towel or cooling rack. Or, hang the long strands on a rack or over the back of a chair, or even on a clothes drying rack. There are a number of interesting commercial pasta drying racks now on the market. It usually takes pasta about 4 to 6 hours to dry.

COOKING PASTA

Start with a large, deep kettle. Use about 6 quarts of water and 2 tablespoons of kosher salt for each pound of pasta. Bring water to a full rolling boil, add salt, and keep it boiling while pasta is cooking. It is not necessary to break long pasta as it will soften and slide into the water (it does make it more manageable to eat, however). Do not cover the pot while cooking pasta. Do not overcook pasta. It should be firm to the bite, but not too chewy. Dried homemade pasta cooks in 5 to 6 minutes. Fresh homemade pasta is usually done in 2 to 3 minutes. Commercial dried pasta generally takes about 8 minutes to cook. Follow the package directions for each variety. The only sure way to tell when pasta is cooked *to the bite* or *al dente* is to periodically fish out a strand and bite it. For homemade fresh pasta, start tasting soon after the water returns to a boil. For commercial dried pasta, start tasting a minute or two before the package directions say it will be done. Stir pasta with a long-handled fork or pasta fork two or three times during the cooking. Drain pasta in a large strainer, or if using a pasta pot with a strainer insert, lift the strainer out of the water and let the water run back into the pot. Do not rinse pasta that will be served hot. Do not allow it to become dry in the strainer, and save a few tablespoons of the cooking water to add to the pasta if it seems dry after it has been sauced. Pour pasta into a warm serving dish and add the sauce, or into the skillet with the sauce, toss to combine and serve immediately.

Keeping cooked pasta hot until serving: Pasta is always best when cooked, drained and sauced immediately before serving. If an unexpected delay occurs, cooked, well-drained pasta can be kept warm for no more than 30 minutes by returning it to the hot cooking pot. Toss with two tablespoons of softened butter or olive oil, cover the pot and place in a "warm" to 200° oven until ready to sauce and serve. Undercook the pasta by a minute or two if you anticipate that serving may be delayed. Unsauced leftover pasta can be reheated by immersing briefly in boiling water immediately prior to saucing. Leftover sauced pasta reheats well in the microwave.

FINEST EGG NOODLES

Rich and golden, these noodles combine a silky smoothness with a delightful texture. They are perfect served with a little melted butter and freshly grated cheese.

2 cups all-purpose flour
½ tsp. salt
½ tsp. dry mustard
1 whole large egg
6 large egg yolks

Mix ingredients by hand, in a heavy-duty mixer, or food processor as directed on pages 9 and 10. Wrap the dough in plastic wrap and allow to rest for at least 20 minutes before rolling and cutting (see pages 11 through 13).

EGG PASTA WITH SEMOLINA FLOUR ^{Makes 1 pound}

Pasta made with semolina flour is perfect for lasagne and cannelloni. The texture is firmer than pasta made only from all-purpose flour. This pasta works best when mixed in a heavy-duty mixer or food processor, and then rolled out in a roller machine.

2 cups semolina flour
1 tsp. salt
1 tbs. olive oil
2 large eggs
2 to 3 tbs. water

Mix ingredients in a heavy-duty mixer or food processor. Wrap the dough in plastic wrap and allow to rest for at least 20 minutes before rolling and cutting (see pages 11 through 13). The dough may seem to be dry and tend to crumble at first, but after a few passes through the machine it will come together.

CARROT PASTA

Carrots add a lovely golden color as well as flavor. This dough is soft enough to be easily rolled out by hand.

½ cup carrot puree (2 to 3 carrots)
2½ cups all-purpose flour
3 large eggs
2 tbs. olive oil
½ tsp. salt
1 to 2 tbs. water as necessary

Peel and cook carrots until very soft. Puree in a blender or food processor. Press puree through a sieve to remove any remaining pieces. Measure out ½ cup puree and return to saucepan. Cook for a minute or two over very low heat to dry out as much as possible. Combine puree with remaining ingredients and continue as directed in basic recipe on page 9. Wrap dough in plastic wrap and allow to rest for at least 20 minutes before rolling and cutting (see pages 11 through 13).

SPINACH PASTA

Makes 1 pound

This beautiful green pasta is delicious with only cheese and butter. Also, try it with any of the vegetable or seafood sauces.

1/2 cup spinach puree (1/2 pkg. frozen spinach)
2 1/2 cups all-purpose flour
3 large eggs
2 tbs. olive oil
1/2 tsp. salt
pinch nutmeg
1 to 2 tbs. water as necessary

Cook spinach and drain very thoroughly. Puree in a blender or food processor. Press through a sieve to remove any bits of stem. Measure out 1/2 cup puree and return to saucepan. Cook for a minute or two over very low heat to dry out as much as possible. Combine with flour, eggs, olive oil, salt and nutmeg. Continue as directed in basic recipe on page 9. Wrap dough in plastic wrap and allow to rest for at least 20 minutes before rolling and cutting (see pages 11 through 13).

SPICY RED PEPPER PASTA

Makes 1 pound

This is a lovely pale pink pasta with a slight tang. Serve with scallops or shrimp for a pretty color and flavor contrast. It also adds a special zest to Fettuccine Alfredo, page 340.

2 tbs. boiling water
2 tsp. dried hot pepper flakes, or to taste
2 cups flour
½ tsp. salt
1 tbs. oil
1 tbs. tomato paste
2 eggs

Put pepper flakes in a small bowl and add boiling water. Let steep for 15 minutes. Combine flour and salt in a food processor bowl and pulse a few times to mix. With processor running, add pepper flakes and water, tomato paste and eggs. Continue as directed in basic recipe on page 9. Wrap dough in plastic wrap and allow to rest for at least 20 minutes before rolling and cutting (see pages 11 through 13).

LEMON PASTA

Here is a light lemony pasta that goes beautifully with seafood or as an accompaniment to spicy dishes in place of rice. It is also delicious in salads.

2 cups all-purpose flour
½ tsp. salt
2 large eggs
2 tbs. vegetable oil
finely grated rind of 1 lemon
¼ cup lemon juice

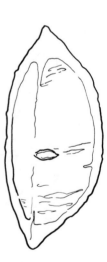

Mix ingredients by hand, in a heavy-duty mixer, or food processor as directed on pages 9 and 10. Wrap dough in plastic wrap and allow to rest for at least 20 minutes before rolling and cutting (see pages 11 through 13).

EXTRA QUICK SAUCES

Here are some extra quick sauces that can be made from start to finish in less time than it takes to boil the water and cook the pasta. All pastas are complemented by a sauce, whether simple or complicated. A little melted butter and some good grated cheese on hot pasta can be just as satisfying as a more elaborate sauce with 20 ingredients that takes more of your time. For a perfect treat anytime, try tossing grated fontina, mozzarella, Gouda or a mild cheddar and two tablespoons melted butter with a hot, well drained pasta. Pasta pairs deliciously with a great variety of cheeses, vegetables, seafood, herbs, nuts and spices.

When making these quick sauces, assemble the ingredients first because there won't be time once you start cooking. Put the appropriate amount of water (at least 6 quarts for 1 pound of pasta) in a large pot and start it heating; then start the sauce. The amount of pasta for a serving, and how much sauce to put on it, is an individual preference. In general, 12 ounces of fresh pasta or 8 ounces of dried pasta will make 3 to 4 medium servings when cooked. Fresh egg pastas have an affinity for sauces based on butter and cheese, while dried pasta shapes adapt well to simple sauces based on olive oil.

Quick pasta dishes can be made from foods you have in your refrigerator (see *Refrigerator Pasta*, page 28). Other fast pasta treats use black olive paste, or sun-dried tomatoes and goat cheese. Or toss cooked pasta with a fresh salsa, hot or mildly spiced. Try some of these sauces and then make your own favorite combinations. Great pasta dishes can be made from good quality ingredients and a little imagination.

PASTA SALSA FRESCA

Preparation time: 15 minutes
Servings: 2 to 3

Take a carton of your favorite fresh salsa from the deli case, hot or mild, toss it with pasta and top with avocado, cheddar cheese, and black olives for a great tasting lunch or supper. Or serve as a side dish with barbecued chicken or fish.

8 oz. dried orecchiette, radiatore or small shell-shaped pasta
12 oz. fresh salsa, hot or mild
1 avocado, peeled and diced
½ cup (2 oz.) coarsely grated cheddar cheese
¼ cup sliced black olives, drained
salt and freshly ground pepper
fresh cilantro for garnish
grated Parmesan cheese

Cook pasta according to package directions. Remove lid from salsa and heat in a microwave for about 45 seconds just to warm salsa, or heat slightly in a small saucepan. When pasta is done, pour into a warm bowl and toss with salsa. Add avocado pieces, cheddar cheese, olives, salt and pepper, and toss again. Top with fresh cilantro leaves and serve. Pass Parmesan cheese.

BLACK OLIVE PASTE
AND ANGEL HAIR PASTA

Preparation time: 15 minutes
Servings: 2

This pasta only takes as long as bringing the pasta water to a boil and cooking the angel hair pasta. Double the recipe for each two people you want to serve. The robust olive paste flavors are a wonderful match for the delicate strands of angel hair pasta. Use the best Parmigiano Reggiano cheese you can buy; it does make a difference. Or, take this on a picnic or to a barbecue — it is delicious at room temperature.

4 oz. dried angel hair pasta
2 tbs. black olive paste
3 tbs. half and half
1/4 tsp. red pepper flakes

freshly ground black pepper
1 large tomato, peeled, seeded, chopped
grated Parmesan cheese

Bring pasta water to a boil. In a warm serving bowl, combine olive paste with half and half. Stir in red pepper flakes and freshly ground black pepper. Add drained cooked pasta to bowl, toss and top with fresh tomato pieces. Pass Parmesan cheese.

PIQUANT PARSLEY SAUCE

Preparation time: 15 minutes
Makes 2/3 cup

This zesty, vibrant no-cook green sauce is terrific on almost any shape of pasta. Let it stand for at least an hour before using. It can be refrigerated for 4 to 5 days, but let it come to room temperature before using with hot pasta.

leaves from 1 bunch Italian parsley (about 2 cups leaves loosely packed)
2 garlic cloves
2 anchovies, drained
2 tbs. capers, drained

⅓ cup full-flavored olive oil
1 tsp. Dijon mustard
2 tbs. ricotta cheese
1 tbs. lemon juice
freshly ground pepper

Using the food processor, with the motor running, drop garlic in feed tube and process until chopped. Add parsley leaves and process until well chopped. Add remaining ingredients and process until well combined but not smooth. Pour into a small bowl, cover and allow to stand for about 1 hour before using.

Or use the blender. Mince garlic and anchovies. Chop parsley by hand. Add olive oil, mustard, ricotta, lemon juice and pepper to blender container and process until well mixed. Add chopped garlic, anchovies, parsley, and capers to oil mixture and blend for a few seconds until well combined, but not smooth. Makes enough sauce for 8 oz. dried or 12 oz. fresh pasta.

PASTA WITH SUN-DRIED TOMATOES AND GARLIC

Preparation time: 20 minutes
Servings: 2

Use the oil packed sun-dried tomatoes with a little of their oil for a full-flavored fast pasta dinner. The angel hair pasta cooks very quickly, 2 to 3 minutes at the most. This recipe can be easily doubled.

4 oz. dried angel hair or capellini shaped pasta

2 tbs. full-flavored olive oil

2 large garlic cloves, minced

2-3 tbs. slivered sun-dried tomatoes

generous amounts of freshly ground black pepper

1/3 cup grated Parmesan cheese

Bring pasta water to a boil. In a medium nonstick skillet sauté garlic 1 to 2 minutes in olive oil and a little sun-dried tomato oil if you have any. Pour cooked pasta into skillet; add garlic, sun-dried tomatoes, black pepper and Parmesan cheese. Toss to combine. Serve immediately on warmed plates. Pass additional Parmesan cheese.

"REFRIGERATOR" PASTA

We amuse our friends with our name for one of our favorites, refrigerator pasta, and we have been encouraged to include it in this book. Here is our outline for a very quick and easy main dish using available ingredients in the refrigerator.

There are a few ingredients that you should always have on hand.

heavy cream (the ultra-pasteurized
    kind will keep for weeks)
good grating cheese
sweet cream butter
fresh garlic
fruity olive oil

tomato paste in a tube
red pepper flakes
yellow or green onions
parsley, especially the flavorful
    Italian flat leaf variety

These ingredients by themselves can be used to make three or four great pasta sauces in the time it takes to boil the pasta water. After you have a base, rummage in the refrigerator and see what else you can find. Look for:

mushrooms
red, green or yellow peppers
ripe tomatoes
leftover vegetables, or easily defrosted
frozen vegetables such as peas

leftover chicken, turkey or ham
tubes of pesto or anchovy paste
soft cheese that can be cubed and
    added to the pasta to melt

If the refrigerator is bare, then look in the cupboard for:

canned chopped clams
canned shrimp, crab or anchovies
canned tuna or salmon
canned mushrooms

canned pimientos or green chiles
chopped olives or olive paste
canned chicken stock or beef broth

Put water on to boil. Based on available ingredients, decide on which pasta shape to cook. Decide whether you will have a cream- or oil-based sauce. Put butter or oil (about a tablespoon per serving of pasta) in a large frying pan and heat on medium. Add a few red pepper flakes, onion or garlic and sauté over medium heat to allow them to release their flavor. When the water boils, add a generous quantity of kosher salt and then the pasta. Stir pasta once or twice to make sure that it doesn't stick together.

Add any ingredients to frying pan that need to be sautéed or cooked. Just before pasta is done, add cream and remaining ingredients and heat through. Drain pasta and add to frying pan. Toss and stir to combine pasta with sauce. Add freshly grated cheese and black pepper if desired. Toss one more time and serve on heated plates. Sprinkle with chopped parsley and some chopped fresh tomato. Pass more cheese at the table.

PASTA WITH GOAT CHEESE AND FRESH TOMATO SAUCE

Preparation time: 15 minutes
Servings: 2

Creamy goat cheese melts into thin strands of angel hair pasta and is garnished with fresh tomato pieces and sweet basil. This pasta cooks fast so prepare the sauce ingredients as the water heats. Double the recipe for more servings.

4 oz. dried angel hair or capellini pasta, or 6 oz. fresh pasta
1 tbs. full-flavored olive oil
4 oz. creamy fresh goat cheese, crumbled
3 fresh Roma or small salad tomatoes, seeded and diced
dash hot pepper flakes
salt and freshly ground pepper
20 fresh sweet basil leaves, cut into slivers

Heat pasta water. Place olive oil and goat cheese in a large warm serving bowl. Pour hot drained pasta into bowl and toss to melt cheese. Add remaining ingredients, toss again, and serve on warm plates.

PASTA WITH CLASSIC
GARLIC AND OIL SAUCE

This is the simplest of all pasta preparations for any kind of pasta. Serve with roasted, broiled or barbecued meats.

12 oz. fresh or 8 oz. dried pasta
1/4 cup fruity olive oil
2 to 3 garlic cloves, finely chopped
3 tbs. chopped fresh sweet basil or 1/2 tsp. dried
1/4 cup chopped parsley, Italian if available
salt and freshly ground black pepper

While pasta is cooking, warm olive oil in a small saucepan. When it is quite warm, remove from heat and add remaining ingredients. The oil should not be so hot that garlic browns. Let steep until pasta is done. Pour hot well-drained pasta into a warmed bowl and toss with sauce. Serve immediately with another grinding of fresh black pepper.

PASTA WITH BUTTER AND CHEESE SAUCE

Preparation time: 15 minutes
Servings: 3 to 4

With only butter and cheese in the refrigerator, you can make this delicious, satisfying sauce. Try it with **Finest Egg Noodles**, *page 16.*

12 oz. fresh or 8 oz. dried pasta
1 stick (¼ lb.) unsalted butter
½ tsp. dried oregano or basil
salt and freshly ground pepper
½ cup freshly grated Parmesan cheese

While pasta is cooking, heat butter gently in a small pan until barely melted. Add herbs, salt and pepper. Pour half the herb-butter into a warm bowl. Add cooked, well-drained pasta and toss quickly. Pour remaining sauce and ½ of the cheese over pasta. Toss until cheese is incorporated and starts to melt. Add remaining cheese and toss until mixed thoroughly. If pasta appears to be dry, add 1 to 2 tbs. of hot pasta cooking water and toss to blend. Serve immediately on warm plates.

Wine suggestion: Pinot Blanc or Napa Gamay

PASTA WITH WHITE WINE AND BUTTER SAUCE

Preparation time: 15 minutes
Servings: 3 to 4

Use this superb sauce alone or with seafood, chicken or vegetables. It has a delightful silky texture and delicate flavor.

12 oz. fresh or 8 oz. dried spaghettini or tagliarini
1/3 cup shallots, minced
2/3 cup dry white wine or dry vermouth
2 tbs. lemon juice

8 tbs. (one stick) unsalted butter
white pepper
2 tbs. minced parsley
6 oz. cooked chicken cut into matchsticks, or shrimp, optional

Have pasta cooking water boiling and ready when needed. Place shallots and white wine in a small heavy saucepan. Reduce wine over high heat until only 2 to 3 tbs. remain. Remove pan from heat and let stand for 3 or 4 minutes. Start pasta cooking. While pasta is cooking, place pan with shallots and wine over very low heat. Add lemon juice. Divide butter into 8 thin slices. Add one butter slice at a time and whisk vigorously until butter is absorbed. Repeat with remaining slices. Remove pan from heat occasionally while beating in the butter. If the pan gets too hot, the butter sauce will separate. Add shrimp or chicken to sauce. Serve over hot, well-drained pasta on warm plates.

Wine suggestion: Chardonnay or Dry Riesling

FETTUCCINE ALFREDO

This recipe for a simple cream and cheese sauce tossed with freshly cooked pasta is a classic.

12 oz. fresh or 8 oz. dried fettuccine
2 tbs. butter
3/4 cup heavy cream
1/2 cup grated Parmesan cheese
freshly grated nutmeg
salt and freshly ground pepper

While pasta is cooking, melt butter in a large skillet. Add cream and 1/4 cup cheese. Simmer over very low heat 4 to 5 minutes until sauce starts to thicken. Drain pasta well and add to skillet. Lift and stir to combine all ingredients and coat pasta. Add remaining cheese, nutmeg, salt and a generous grinding of black pepper. Serve on warm plates.

Variation: Add 1/4 tsp. hot pepper flakes to skillet when butter has melted.

PASTA WITH ZESTY TOMATO AND HOT PEPPER SAUCE

Preparation time: 15 minutes
Servings: 3 to 4

For the very best flavor, use fresh Romano tomatoes if they are available, or small regular tomatoes.

8 oz. dried or 12 oz. fresh fettuccine or tagliarini
6 to 8 Romano tomatoes, peeled
1/4 cup fruity olive oil
2 tsp. minced garlic
1 tsp. fresh oregano, or 1/2 tsp. dried
1 to 2 small fresh hot peppers, finely chopped
salt and freshly ground pepper
freshly grated Parmesan cheese

While pasta is cooking, cut tomatoes in quarters and remove seeds. Heat olive oil in a large skillet. When hot, add tomatoes, garlic, oregano, hot peppers, salt and pepper. Sauté over medium heat 4 or 5 minutes, or until tomatoes are soft but still hold their shape. Toss with hot well-drained pasta in a warm bowl. Serve immediately. Pass Parmesan cheese.

PASTA WITH FRESH TOMATO AND GARLIC SAUCE

Preparation time: 15 minutes
Servings: 3 to 4

Make this uncooked sauce at least one hour before serving and allow it to stand at room temperature to develop the flavors.

8 oz. dried or 12 oz. fresh spaghetti or tagliarini
3 large ripe tomatoes, peeled, seeded and coarsely chopped
2 tbs. chopped fresh sweet basil
1 tbs. chopped fresh chives
2 tbs. chopped Italian flat-leaf parsley or cilantro

3 garlic cloves, finely chopped
2 tbs. fruity olive oil
½ cup finely grated mozzarella or fontina cheese
salt and freshly ground pepper
freshly grated Parmesan cheese

Combine tomatoes, basil, chives, parsley, garlic, olive oil, cheese, salt and pepper in a medium-size bowl. Let stand approximately 1 hour before serving. Cook pasta. Combine sauce and hot pasta in a warm bowl. Pass Parmesan cheese.

PASTA WITH CLASSIC PESTO SAUCE

Preparation time: 20 minutes
Servings: 4 to 5

Fragrant fresh sweet basil leaves, garlic, pine nuts or walnuts and olive oil make a delicious sauce for homemade pasta.

1 lb. fresh pasta or 12 oz. dried pasta
2 cups fresh basil leaves
3 large garlic cloves
3/4 cup pine nuts or chopped walnuts

3/4 cup fruity olive oil
3/4 cup freshly grated Parmesan cheese
1/2 tsp. salt, or to taste
freshly ground pepper

While pasta is cooking, place fresh basil leaves, garlic, nuts and olive oil in a food processor bowl or blender container. Process until ingredients are well mixed, scraping down sides of container once or twice. Process until mixture is fairly smooth. Pour into a bowl and stir in cheese, salt and pepper. Toss with hot, well-drained pasta in a warm bowl.

Variation: Cook 1 cup rizo or other rice-shaped pasta according to package directions. Stir in 1/3 cup pesto sauce. Fill 4 hollowed-out, medium tomatoes with mixture. Top with Parmesan cheese and bake in a 375° oven 15 minutes. Serve hot with barbecued lamb or steaks.

PASTA WITH CREAMY NUT SAUCE

Preparation time: 15 minutes
Servings: 3 to 4

*Serve over small shells or bowties, or with **Cheese Ravioli**, page 146.*

12 oz. fresh pasta or 8 oz. dried pasta
2 tbs. butter
1 large garlic clove, minced
2 tbs. flour
1⅓ cups Swanson's beef or chicken broth

½ tsp. anchovy paste
¼ tsp. white pepper
¼ tsp. salt
1 cup very finely chopped walnuts
⅓ cup heavy cream
parsley for garnish

While pasta is cooking, melt butter in a small saucepan. Sauté garlic for 1 minute. Add flour and cook 2 minutes. Gradually add broth, anchovy paste, pepper and salt. Cook until sauce thickens. Stir in walnuts and cream just before serving. Cook just long enough to heat sauce. Toss with hot, well-drained pasta in a warm bowl. Sprinkle with chopped parsley.

Wine suggestion: Dry Riesling

PASTA WITH SPICY PEPPERONI AND MUSHROOM SAUCE

Preparation time: 15 minutes
Servings: 3 to 4

This hearty sauce is perfect when you're hungry, but short on time.

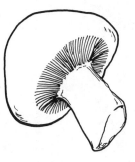

12 oz. fresh pasta or 8 oz. dried pasta
1 tbs. oil
1/4 lb. pepperoni, skin removed and thinly sliced
1/2 lb. fresh mushrooms, thinly sliced
4 to 5 green onions
1/2 cup heavy cream
salt and freshly ground pepper

While pasta is cooking, heat oil in a large skillet. Sauté pepperoni 3 to 4 minutes. Remove and set aside. Add sliced mushrooms and onions to skillet. Sauté 4 to 5 minutes over medium heat until mushrooms are limp and onions are soft. Add cream, pepperoni, salt and pepper; heat through. Combine with hot, well-drained pasta and serve immediately on warm plates.

Wine suggestion: Barbera or full-bodied Zinfandel

SPAGHETTI CARBONARA

Preparation time: 20 minutes
Servings: 4 to 5

Here is a classic sauce with bacon, eggs and cream. If it is available, the Italian rolled bacon called pancetta will add special character and flavor to this dish.

1 lb. fresh pasta or 12 oz. dried pasta
½ lb. bacon or pancetta, thinly sliced
1 large onion, chopped
½ cup finely chopped parsley
2 eggs, room temperature

¾ cup freshly grated Parmesan cheese
¼ tsp. hot pepper flakes, optional
½ cup heavy cream

Start heating pasta cooking water so it will be ready when needed. Cut bacon into 1-inch pieces. Sauté in skillet until crisp. Remove bacon pieces. Pour off all but 2 tbs. bacon fat. Sauté onion in bacon fat 3 to 4 minutes until soft. Combine parsley, eggs, Parmesan cheese, pepper flakes and cream in a small mixing bowl. Cook pasta and drain well. Place pasta in a large warm bowl. Quickly pour egg mixture over hot pasta and mix. Add bacon and onion. Toss to combine. Serve immediately on warm plates.

Wine suggestion: a light, fruity Zinfandel or Napa Gamay

SAVORY APPETIZERS AND SOUPS

While pasta was probably known in Italy long before Marco Polo returned from China, the Chinese have had several hundred years' more experience with both boiled and fried pasta. Most supermarkets carry several different sizes of fresh Asian noodles, 3-inch square or round won ton wrappers, and the larger egg roll wrappers. These fresh noodles and wrappers can be used interchangeably in most pasta recipes. The Asian noodles cook very quickly, 2 to 3 minutes, and can be drained, and then covered with cool water until you are ready to use them. The won ton wrappers can be filled and fried or boiled, and also make wonderful small ravioli.

Fried won ton appetizers can be made ahead, lightly browned in oil, cooled and then frozen in airtight containers. When you are ready to serve them, place on a rack in a shallow pan and bake in a 350° oven 10 to 15 minutes until hot and crisp. We have included a traditional filling with pork, shrimp and water chestnuts, as well as a *Green Chile and Cheese* recipe. The *Goat Cheese and Sun-dried Tomato* ravioli filling, page 142, also makes a delicious fried won ton.

Jumbo cooked pasta shells are filled with a *Spicy Chicken or Shrimp Salad* for a make-ahead appetizer. Or stuff them with your favorite tuna or chunky cooked vegetable salad and take them for lunch or on a picnic.

Pasta soups range from light to hearty and we have included a few of each. The *Cold Lemon Pasta Soup*, *Pasta in Broth* and the *Green Chile Pasta Soup* all make delicious starters for a dinner. The *Pasta and Bean Soup*, and the *Mushroom Pasta Soup* can be used as the entrée for a soup and salad meal.

SPICY CHICKEN SHELLS

Preparation time: 20 minutes
Makes: 8

Consider using smoked turkey or chicken, or turkey ham in place of the cooked chicken. This recipe is easily doubled or tripled. If you make them ahead, remember to take them out of the refrigerator about 15 minutes before serving. Cook 2-3 extra shells in case some split during cooking.

8-10 jumbo dried pasta shells
2 oz. light cream cheese
1/4 cup prepared chunky salsa, hot or mild
1 tbs. chopped fresh cilantro

2 tbs. almonds, toasted, coarsely chopped, or pine nuts, toasted
1 cup diced cooked chicken
salt and freshly ground pepper
fresh cilantro leaves for garnish

Cook pasta shells according to package directions. Drain immediately and rinse with cold water. Combine cream cheese, salsa, chopped cilantro and almonds. Mix well. Add diced chicken, salt and pepper. Stuff drained and dried pasta shells. Garnish each shell with fresh whole cilantro leaf. Refrigerate if not serving immediately.

SHRIMP SALAD SHELLS

Preparation time: 20 minutes
Makes: 12

These light appetizers go beautifully with a crisp Pinot Grigio or a dry riesling. Or serve them as part of a luncheon or picnic plate with ripe red tomatoes and a vegetable salad. Cook a couple of extra shells in case some of them split during cooking.

12-15 dried jumbo shells
4 green onions, thinly sliced
1/4 cup finely diced celery
1/4 cup finely minced fresh parsley
2 tbs. finely chopped sun-dried tomato pieces, oil packed

2 tsp. lemon juice
1 tbs. light cream cheese
1 tbs. reduced calorie mayonnaise
1 lb. small cooked salad shrimp
salt and finely ground white pepper

Cook pasta shells according to package directions. Drain and rinse with cold water to keep them from sticking and to cool them before stuffing. Save 12 small whole shrimp for garnish. If shrimp are 1 inch to 1½ inches in size, cut each in half. Combine remaining ingredients and mix lightly with a fork. Fill pasta shells with a small spoon and refrigerate until ready to serve. Garnish each with reserved whole shrimp. These are best eaten the day you make them.

APPETIZER WON TON

Preparation time: 45 minutes
Makes: 50 to 60

Won ton can be fried for appetizers or simmered in broth for a hearty soup.

½ lb. ground pork
2 tsp. cornstarch
1 tbs. soy sauce
2 tsp. dry sherry
1 tsp. sesame oil
1 tbs. vegetable oil
salt and pepper

4 small fresh shrimp, finely chopped
1 egg white
4 green onions, finely chopped
6 water chestnuts, finely chopped
50 to 60 won ton wrappers
oil for frying

Combine pork, cornstarch, soy sauce, sherry and sesame oil. Heat vegetable oil in a skillet. Fry pork mixture 4 to 5 minutes, crumbling meat as it cooks. Remove meat from skillet with a slotted spoon or drain in a sieve to remove fat. Place meat in a bowl. Add salt, pepper and shrimp. Stir in egg white, onions and chestnuts. Place 1 teaspoon filling in center of a won ton wrapper. (Keep unused wrappers covered with a damp towel.) Moisten one-half of wrapper edge with water. Fold over to form a triangle, pressing firmly around edges to seal. Moisten left tip of triangle. Bring right tip to meet it and press tips together. Heat oil to 375°. Fry won ton a few at a time until lightly browned. Drain on paper towels. Serve immediately.

GREEN CHILE AND CHEESE APPETIZERS

Preparation time: 45 minutes
Makes: 50 to 60

Won ton wrappers are used for this quick appetizer. Make these ahead and keep them in the freezer until ready to reheat and serve.

2 tbs. canned green chiles, seeded and finely chopped
1 cup grated Parmesan cheese
4 oz. cream cheese
1 egg yolk
50 to 60 won ton wrappers
oil for frying
mild taco sauce for dipping

Combine chiles, Parmesan, cream cheese and egg yolk. Chill in refrigerator 20 to 30 minutes for easier handling. Fill won ton wrappers according to directions for *Appetizer Won Ton* on page 45. Heat oil to 375°. Fry won ton a few at a time until very lightly browned. Drain on paper towels. Serve immediately with a mild taco sauce for dipping.

PASTA AND BEAN SOUP

Preparation time: 45 minutes
Makes: 50 to 60

This hearty nutritious soup is especially good in cold weather. Add a green salad and some garlic bread to make a satisfying meal.

2 tbs. light olive oil
1 small onion, diced
1 large carrot, diced
1 celery stalk, diced
1 large can (49½ oz.) clear chicken broth
3 tbs. tomato paste
2 cans (15 oz. each) cannellini beans
4 oz. pasta shells or macaroni
grated Parmesan cheese

Heat olive oil in a large saucepan. Add onion, celery and carrot and cook over low heat 3 to 4 minutes until vegetables have softened, but not browned. Add chicken broth and tomato paste and simmer over medium high heat for 15 minutes. Puree one can of beans in a food processor or blender until smooth and add to saucepan. Add pasta and simmer until it is almost cooked. Add second can of beans and continue cooking until pasta is tender. Taste carefully for salt and add generous grinds of black pepper. Serve immediately. Pass grated Parmesan cheese.

HONG KONG NOODLE SOUP

Preparation time: 20 minutes
Servings: 4

Serve soup as a light lunch or follow with a stir-fry dish for a Chinese-style dinner.

8 oz. fresh Chinese-style noodles or 4 oz. dried noodles
2 cans (14 oz. each) chicken or beef broth
½ tsp. sesame oil
1 tbs. soy sauce
white pepper
½ cup diced cooked ham, chicken, pork or shrimp
½ cup frozen peas
5 green onions with 1 inch of green top, thinly sliced

Cook noodles in a large pot of rapidly boiling water for 3 minutes. Drain well. Bring broth to boil in a large saucepan. Add drained noodles, sesame oil, soy sauce, white pepper, diced meat, peas and green onions. Cook 5 minutes. Serve immediately.

Variation: Add 1 cup coarsely chopped fresh spinach leaves in place of peas. Cook until leaves wilt.

WON TON SOUP

Preparation time: 45 minutes
Cooking time: 15 minutes
Servings: 4

Prepare the won ton as directed on page 45. Instead of frying them all, drop 20 to 25 won ton in this rich broth for a delicious, hearty soup.

4 cups chicken or beef broth
1 tbs. soy sauce
½ tsp. sesame oil
3 green onions, finely chopped
½ tsp. pepper
20 to 25 filled won ton
½ cup frozen peas
½ cup diced cooked carrot

Bring broth to a boil. Add soy sauce, sesame oil, onions and pepper. Reduce heat to simmer and add won ton. Gently simmer, uncovered, for 12 to 14 minutes. During the last 6 minutes of cooking, add peas and carrots. Serve in soup bowls, ladling 5 to 6 won ton into each bowl with broth.

PASTA IN BROTH

Preparation time: 30 minutes
Servings: 4

If you don't have homemade broth available, here is a delicious substitute. Add pasta and you have a light soup.

2 cans (15 oz. each) beef or chicken broth (or use one of each)
½ cup finely chopped onion
½ cup finely chopped carrot
¼ cup finely chopped celery, including some leaves
1 bay leaf
2 or 3 black peppercorns
2 oz. dried thin pasta, riso, shells or other small shapes

Combine broth, onion, carrot, celery and seasonings in a medium-sized saucepan. Bring to a boil and gently simmer, uncovered, for 20 minutes. Strain through a sieve or damp cheesecloth, pressing as much juice as possible out of the vegetables. Discard vegetables. Measure stock. If necessary, add enough water to bring stock up to 4 cups. Return to saucepan. Bring to a boil. Add thin pasta broken into 1-inch pieces, or riso, alphabets, or other small pasta. Cook until pasta is done. Serve immediately in warm bowls.

LEMON PASTA SOUP

Preparation time: 15 minutes
Servings: 6

This soup can be served hot or cold, but it is particularly nice chilled and served in pretty glass bowls. Garnish with thin lemon slices.

1/2 cup tiny pasta shapes (stars or shells)
6 cups chicken broth
salt to taste

1/8 tsp. white pepper
3 eggs
1/3 cup lemon juice
1 lemon, thinly sliced for garnish

Combine pasta, chicken broth, salt and pepper in a saucepan. Bring to a boil. Cover and simmer until pasta is tender, about 10 minutes. Remove from heat. Beat eggs in a separate bowl until pale yellow. Slowly add lemon juice to eggs. Carefully stir some of the hot broth into the egg-lemon mixture, beating continuously. Add tempered egg-lemon mixture to remaining hot broth. If serving hot, ladle into hot soup cups and garnish with lemon. If serving cold, cool soup and refrigerate 3 to 4 hours or overnight. Serve very cold and stir well before ladling into serving bowls. Garnish each bowl with one or two thin lemon slices.

MUSHROOM PASTA SOUP

Preparation time: 45
Servings: 4

*This flavorful soup uses both fresh and dried Oriental mushrooms for a rich taste.
Use a food processor to chop the vegetables and slice the mushrooms.*

2 oz. dried pasta (small shells, small macaroni or noodles)
2 dried Oriental mushrooms
3 cans (15 oz. each) beef broth
½ cup finely chopped onion
½ cup finely chopped carrot
¼ cup finely chopped celery, including some leaves
1 bay leaf
2 or 3 black peppercorns
2 tbs. butter
½ lb. fresh mushrooms, thinly sliced
2 tbs. brandy
⅛ tsp. white pepper

Cook pasta according to package directions. Rinse with cold water, drain and set aside. Cover dried mushrooms with boiling water and let stand for 20 minutes. Drain and squeeze mushrooms dry. Cut mushrooms into small squares, discarding the hard stem. In a large saucepan, combine beef broth, onion, carrot, celery, bay leaf and peppercorns. Bring to a boil and simmer, uncovered, for 20 minutes. Strain broth through a sieve or damp cheesecloth, pressing as much juice as possible out of the vegetables. Discard vegetables. Return broth to saucepan. Heat butter in a large skillet. When foaming, add fresh mushrooms and the dried mushroom pieces. Sauté over high heat 3 to 4 minutes until mushrooms are almost done. Pour brandy over mushrooms and continue to cook for another minute until mushrooms are fairly dry. Season with white pepper. Approximately 10 minutes before serving, add mushrooms to broth and bring to a boil. Add pasta and heat through. Serve in hot soup bowls garnished with parsley.

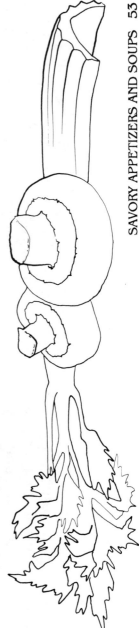

GREEN CHILE PASTA SOUP

Preparation time: 30 minutes
Servings: 3 to 4

Creamy and mildly spicy, this makes a delicious winter soup.

3 oz. thin pasta or small shells
1 tbs. butter
6 green onions, thinly sliced
2 canned green chiles, or to taste
1 can (14 oz.) chicken broth

½ tsp. ground cumin
salt
¼ tsp. white pepper
1 cup half and half
cilantro or chopped pimiento

Cook pasta according to package directions (if using thin pasta, break in 1-inch pieces). Drain. Heat butter in a small skillet. Sauté onions until soft. Drain green chiles and remove seeds. Place chiles, sautéed onion and a little of the chicken broth in a food processor bowl or blender container and process until mixture is smooth. Bring chicken broth to a boil in a medium saucepan. Add chile mixture, cumin, salt, pepper and cooked pasta. Add light cream and heat through. Pour into warm soup bowls and garnish with cilantro or pimiento. Serve immediately.

INNOVATIVE PASTA SALADS

Pasta salads make splendid side dishes for chicken, fish, ham or other meat entrées. They can also be the featured dish for luncheons, picnics and cold suppers.

The only time hot cooked pasta is drained and rinsed with cold water is when it is going to be used for a salad. This step cools the pasta before it is combined with the dressing and other ingredients. It is also important to toss the drained pasta immediately with a tablespoon of oil or some of the dressing to keep it from sticking together.

Tender, delicately flavored pasta complements the crisp, colorful vegetable pieces and slivers of meat that are often used in salads. The most piquant dressings are quickly absorbed and become wonderfully mellow as they chill. Remember to prepare most pasta salads 1 to 2 hours ahead so they can chill and the flavors have time to harmonize. Stir the salads after an hour or so of chilling. If they appear dry, add a little more mayonnaise or oil to moisten. Salads should be removed from the refrigerator 15 to 20 minutes before serving so the ingredients are not icy cold. Salads should be garnished with parsley, cilantro or other toppings just before serving. If salads are to be served outside it is important to keep them as cold as possible and out of the sun to avoid spoilage.

This section features many easy and quick salads including a springtime pairing of asparagus and oranges, cumin- and chile-flavored couscous salad, *Bangkok Noodle Salad* with a creamy peanut dressing, hearty *Deli Salad* made with cold cuts, a *Hot Dogs and Wagonwheels Salad* that appeals to the younger set, and many other combinations.

BLUE CHEESE PASTA SALAD

Preparation time: 15 minutes
Servings: 8

This salad is nice as a cheese course. Use Danish Blue, Roquefort, Stilton, or any blue-veined cheese. Make salad 1 to 2 hours ahead so flavors have time to develop.

12 oz. fresh pasta or 8 oz. dried pasta (corkscrews, wagon wheels or small shells)

4 oz. blue-veined cheese, crumbled

2 cups walnuts, toasted and coarsely chopped

1 cup chopped celery

4 tbs. mayonnaise

⅛ tsp. white pepper

salt

3 tbs. minced parsley

Cook pasta as directed. Immediately rinse with cold water and drain well. Add cheese, walnuts, celery, mayonnaise, pepper and salt. Gently toss with two forks until ingredients are well mixed. Refrigerate 1 to 2 hours. Add a little more mayonnaise if salad seems dry. Sprinkle with parsley. Serve slightly chilled.

Wine suggestion: Cabernet

CELERY ROOT AND PASTA SALAD

Preparation time: 30 minutes
Servings: 3 to 4

Use spinach pasta for a pretty contrast with the white celery root and carrot strips. Add strips of prosciutto or salami for variation. The best celery roots are about 4 inches in diameter. The larger ones sometimes have soft centers.

4 oz. spinach linguine
2 tbs. Dijon mustard
3 tbs. rice wine vinegar
⅓ cup olive oil
salt and freshly ground pepper
1 cup celery root, peeled, cut in julienne strips
1 large or 2 small carrots, cut into 3-inch long by ¼-inch matchsticks
4 oz. provolone or smoked Gouda cheese, cut into thin strips
¼ cup Italian parsley, finely chopped

Bring pasta water to a boil. Break linguine strands into thirds. Add to pasta water and cook. About 2 minutes before pasta is done, add carrot strips to pot. Make dressing by whisking together mustard and vinegar in a large bowl. Slowly add oil and continue to whisk until mixture thickens.

Season with salt and pepper. Peel celery root, cut into thin slices and then into julienne strips, or use the julienne blade in the food processor. The celery root should be added to the dressing as soon as possible so it does not turn brown.

Combine cooked pasta and carrots with dressing and celery root mixture. Cool for about 10 to 15 minutes before adding cheese strips and parsley. This can be refrigerated for several hours before serving.

ASPARAGUS AND
ORANGE PASTA SALAD

Preparation time: 30 minutes
Servings: 3 to 4

This salad is the essence of spring with delicious young asparagus and orange segments tossed with pasta. The orange zest adds some zip to the mayonnaise dressing.

16 thin fresh asparagus spears
1 tbs. full-flavored olive oil
1 medium leek, white part only
2 garlic cloves, minced
1 tbs. grated fresh ginger
dash red pepper flakes
2 small oranges
8 oz. gemellini or corkscrew-shaped pasta
1/2 cup reduced calorie mayonnaise
salt and white pepper

Bring pasta water to a boil. Cut asparagus spears on the diagonal into 1/2-inch-thick slices. Cut leek into strips 1/4-inch wide by 2 inches long. Place in a sieve and rinse well to get rid of any sand. Heat olive oil in a small nonstick skillet. Sauté leeks, ginger, garlic and red pepper flakes over low heat about 10 minutes, until leeks are soft but not brown.

Using a fine grater, grate rind from both oranges. Stir rind into mayonnaise. Carefully cut remaining rind and membrane from oranges and segment oranges. Squeeze any remaining juice from membrane into mayonnaise.

Cook pasta according to package directions. About 2 minutes before pasta is done, add asparagus pieces. When pasta is cooked, drain well and rinse with cold water. Toss pasta and asparagus in a large bowl with leek and garlic mixture. Cool for 10 to 15 minutes before adding mayonnaise. Toss with mayonnaise and orange segments. Chill for 1 to 2 hours before serving.

GARDEN VEGETABLE PASTA SALAD

Preparation time: 30 minutes
Servings: 4

Crisp fresh vegetable pieces accent radiatore, gemellini, fusilli or the pasta shape of your choice. If you make this more than a few hours before serving, add the julienned fresh sweet basil just before serving. Add a cup of diced cooked chicken, ham or salad shrimp for a nice variation.

8 oz. dried radiatore, gemellini or
   fusilli
1 tbs. full-flavored olive oil
¼ cup finely chopped red onion
½ medium sweet red, green or
   yellow pepper, diced
1 celery stalk, thinly sliced
1 small carrot, coarsely grated
1 medium tomato, peeled, seeded,
   chopped

dash red pepper flakes
1 tsp. Dijon mustard
3 tbs. full-flavored olive oil
1 tbs. rice wine vinegar
1 tsp. lemon juice
salt and freshly ground pepper
¼ cup grated Parmesan cheese
¼ cup fresh sweet basil, julienned

Bring pasta water to a boil and cook pasta. Immediately rinse with cold water, drain and toss in a large mixing bowl with 1 tbs. olive oil. Add onion, pepper, celery, carrot, tomato and red pepper flakes. In a small bowl, whisk together Dijon mustard, 3 tbs. olive oil, rice wine vinegar, lemon juice, salt and pepper. When mixture forms an emulsion, add to pasta and vegetables. Toss to combine. Pour into a serving bowl; top with Parmesan cheese and sweet basil. This salad can be served immediately or refrigerated 1 to 2 hours or overnight before serving.

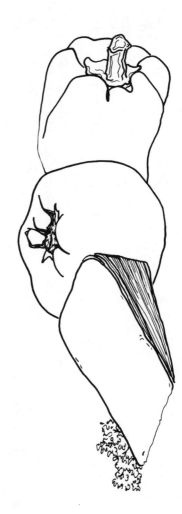

SOUTH OF THE BORDER
COUSCOUS SALAD

Preparation time: 30 minutes
Servings: 3 to 4

This light salad is full of zesty flavors of cumin, chile powder, and peppers, garnished with tomato and avocado. It is best served the same day it is made. Serve with crisp tortilla chips.

¾ cup water
1 tbs. vegetable oil
½ cup quick cooking couscous
1 tbs. light vegetable oil
3-4 green onions, thinly sliced
½ cup diced red or green peppers
1 garlic clove, minced
¼ tsp. chile powder
1 tsp. cumin
½ tsp. dried oregano

1 small jalapeño pepper, minced, or to taste
½ cup peeled, diced jicama
1 ripe avocado, peeled and diced
1 large, ripe tomato, peeled, seeded and chopped
2 tsp. lime juice
¼ cup fresh cilantro leaves for garnish

Bring water and oil to a boil in a medium saucepan or skillet. Pour in couscous, stir, remove from heat, cover and let stand for 5 minutes. Fluff with a fork and pour into a mixing bowl so mixture can cool before adding remaining ingredients.

Heat 1 tbs. oil in a nonstick skillet. Sauté green onions, peppers, garlic, chile powder, cumin, oregano and jalapeño pepper over low heat 3 to 4 minutes until onion softens. Add to couscous mixture. Prepare remaining ingredients. Stir in jicama, avocado, tomato and lime juice. Top with fresh cilantro leaves and serve. Salad can be prepared and refrigerated for 1 to 2 hours before serving. Add avocado and fresh cilantro just before serving.

TORTELLINI AND ARTICHOKE SALAD

Preparation time: 20 minutes
Servings: 6 appetizer or
3 to 4 luncheon

Here is a fast appetizer or luncheon salad using deli ingredients. Pick up some tortellini, marinated artichoke hearts, pimiento or roasted red peppers and add a dressing.

1 pkg. (10 oz.) fresh cheese or chicken tortellini
3-4 marinated artichoke hearts or bottoms
2-3 tbs. diced roasted red peppers or pimento
4 tbs. reduced calorie mayonnaise
2 tsp. Dijon mustard
1 tbs. grated Parmesan cheese
salt
white pepper
2 tbs. fresh sweet basil, cut into slivers, or ½ tsp. dried
2 tbs. chopped Italian parsley

Cook tortellini as directed on package. Rinse with cold water and drain well. Toss with 1 tbs. marinated artichoke liquid to keep from sticking together. Allow tortellini to cool while preparing rest of ingredients. Drain artichokes. Cut artichoke bottoms into 1/4-inch slivers, and artichoke hearts into small pieces. Combine cooled tortellini, artichokes, red peppers with mayonnaise, mustard, salt and pepper. Refrigerate if not serving immediately. Garnish with fresh basil and parsley just before serving.

Variation: Add 1/2 cup small, cooked shrimp or thin strips of prosciutto.

Note: If using fresh cooked artichokes, add 1 tbs. olive oil to coat the tortellini after it has been cooked and drained.

BANGKOK NOODLE SALAD

Preparation time: 30 minutes
Servings: 3 to 4

Chunky peanut butter dressing, slivered cucumber, chicken, carrots and thin pasta strands topped with crunchy chopped peanuts make a great lunch or picnic salad. Allow to rest an hour before serving for flavors to combine. This is best made and eaten the same day.

4 oz. dried capellini or 6 oz. fresh thin pasta
4 green onions, white part only, thinly sliced
½ cup coarsely grated or thinly sliced carrot
½ cup cucumber, cut into thin strips
1 cup cooked chicken, cut into thin strips
½ cup fresh cilantro leaves and chopped peanuts for garnish

Break pasta strands in half and cook pasta according to package directions. Rinse with cold water and drain well. Pour into a large bowl and toss with dressing. Add carrots, cucumber and chicken strips. Toss to combine. Refrigerate 1 hour before serving. Garnish with fresh cilantro and chopped peanuts.

Dressing

1/4 cup chunky peanut butter
2 tbs. soy sauce
1 tsp. Dijon mustard
1/4 tsp. red pepper flakes
2 tbs. rice wine vinegar
2 tsp. sesame oil

Combine in a small bowl and stir until thick and creamy.

SESAME NOODLE SALAD

Preparation time: 30 minutes
Servings: 3 to 4

The fresh thin Chinese or Hong Kong style noodles used in this dish can often be found in the supermarket produce or dairy section. If you cut the noodle package in half before cooking, the noodles will be more manageable. Substitute capellini or spaghetti if these noodles are not available.

8 oz. fresh Chinese-style noodles, or 6 oz. dried pasta
1 tbs. sesame oil
2 tbs. rice wine vinegar
1 tbs. vegetable oil
2 tbs. soy sauce
2 garlic cloves, minced
¼ tsp. red pepper flakes
2 green onions, thinly sliced
2 oz. fresh snow peas, blanched, cut into thin strips
1 large carrot, coarsely grated
½ cup firm tofu, cut into thin strips, optional
1 tbs. toasted sesame seeds
fresh cilantro leaves for garnish

Cook noodles as directed on package, approximately 1 to 3 minutes for fresh noodles. Drain and rinse with cold water, drain again and place in a large mixing bowl. Toss immediately with 1 tbs. sesame oil to keep noodles from sticking together. Combine wine vinegar, vegetable oil, soy sauce, garlic and red pepper flakes in a small microwavable bowl. Heat on high, uncovered, for 30 seconds. Or bring to a boil in a small saucepan and cook for 1 minute.

Combine wine vinegar mixture with cooked noodles, toss and add onions, snow peas and shredded carrot. If not serving immediately, refrigerate. Just before serving, toss with toasted sesame seeds and top with tofu strips and fresh cilantro leaves.

Variation: Substitute 1/2 cup small cooked shrimp and 1 cup finely diced celery for tofu. Or substitute 1 cup finely shredded red cabbage for tofu.

PATIO SHELL SALAD

This hearty salad features red kidney beans, yellow corn, green chiles and cumin for a South-of-the-border flavor. Serve with grilled meat.

4 oz. dried small pasta shells
1 can (15 oz.) red kidney beans, well drained
1 can (12 oz.) corn, well drained
4 to 5 green onions, finely chopped
4 to 5 tbs. finely chopped canned green chiles

½ tsp. ground cumin
1 tsp. dried oregano
1 tbs. lemon juice
½ cup mayonnaise
½ tsp. salt
¼ tsp. freshly ground black pepper

Cook pasta according to package directions. Immediately rinse with cold water and drain well. Rinse kidney beans under cold water and drain well. Rinse corn and drain. Combine pasta, kidney beans, corn, onions, chiles, cumin, oregano, lemon juice, mayonnaise, salt and pepper. Gently toss with two forks. Chill in refrigerator for at least 2 hours before serving. Add a little more mayonnaise if pasta seems dry.

Wine suggestion: Gewurztraminer

MACARONI SALAD

Preparation time: 30 minutes
Servings: 4 to 6

This is a perfect picnic salad. For even better flavor, make it a few hours ahead and let it mellow in the refrigerator before serving.

1 cup uncooked salad macaroni
2 hard-cooked eggs, chopped
1 tbs. minced green onion
1/4 cup minced sweet pickle
1/4 cup finely diced celery
1 tbs. capers
1 cup cooked green peas
2 tbs. chopped pimiento

1/2 cup mayonnaise
2 tbs. pickle juice
1 tsp. prepared mustard
1/4 tsp. white pepper
1 tsp. salt
2 tbs. sour cream
2 tbs. minced parsley

Cook macaroni in boiling water for 12 minutes, or according to package directions. Immediately rinse with cold water and drain well. Place in a mixing bowl. Add chopped eggs, onion, pickle, celery, capers, peas and pimiento. Combine mayonnaise, pickle juice, mustard, pepper, salt and sour cream. Add to macaroni mixture. Add parsley. Toss lightly with two forks to combine. Chill before serving.

PASTA SALAD WITH GREEN BEANS AND WALNUTS

Preparation time: 15 minutes
Servings: 4 to 6

This hearty salad makes a great luncheon main course or serve it on the buffet table.

8 oz. corkscrew pasta
3 cups cooked fresh green beans
1 cup coarsely chopped walnuts
4 tbs. olive oil
2 tbs. white wine vinegar
⅛ tsp. cayenne

1 cup diced ham or salami
4 green onions, thinly sliced
2 tbs. minced parsley
1 tbs. dried dill weed or 3 to 4 tbs. fresh dill, finely chopped
salt to taste

Cook pasta, drain and immediately rinse with cold water. Drain well and pour into a large bowl. Cut green beans in 1-inch pieces. Toss with pasta. Toast chopped walnuts in oven until hot to the touch. Combine olive oil, white wine vinegar and cayenne. Pour over pasta and green beans. Gently toss with 2 forks. Add ham, walnuts, onions, parsley, dill weed and salt. Toss well. Serve at room temperature or slightly chilled.

HOT DOGS AND WAGONWHEELS

Preparation time: 30 minutes
Servings: 4 to 6

This is a whimsical salad that is a sure hit with the kids. It makes great picnic fare.

6 oz. wagonwheel pasta
5 all-beef hot dogs, boiled and sliced into thin rounds
1/3 cup thinly sliced sweet pickle
1/4 cup finely chopped green pepper
2 green onions, white part only, thinly sliced
1/2 cup mayonnaise
1 tbs. prepared mustard
2 tsp. cider vinegar
salt and pepper to taste
2 tbs. chopped parsley

Cook wagonwheels according to package directions. Drain and immediately rinse with cold water. Drain again well. Place hot dogs and pasta in large bowl. Add pickle, green pepper, green onions, mayonnaise, mustard, vinegar, salt, pepper and parsley. Gently toss with two forks. Chill in refrigerator at least 2 hours.

DELI PASTA SALAD

Preparation time: 30 minutes
Servings: 4 entrée or
6 to 8 first course

This hearty salad is easily assembled from ingredients purchased at the deli.

8 oz. dried egg noodles
3 oz. mortadella, bologna or ham, thinly sliced
3 oz. Gruyére or Swiss cheese, thinly sliced
1 large sour or German-style pickle
1 large or 2 small tart apples, peeled and cored
1½ tbs. Worcestershire sauce
3 to 4 tbs. mayonnaise
½ tsp. white pepper
2 tbs. freshly grated Parmesan cheese
2 tbs. parsley, minced

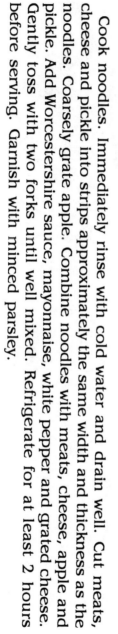

Cook noodles. Immediately rinse with cold water and drain well. Cut meats, cheese and pickle into strips approximately the same width and thickness as the noodles. Coarsely grate apple. Combine noodles with meats, cheese, apple and pickle. Add Worcestershire sauce, mayonnaise, white pepper and grated cheese. Gently toss with two forks until well mixed. Refrigerate for at least 2 hours before serving. Garnish with minced parsley.

PASTA WITH FRESH VEGETABLES

Vegetables with pasta make an attractive combination that offers a delicious contrast of textures and is very pleasing to the eye. Red, green and yellow peppers, orange carrots, yellow and green squash, red tomatoes, green asparagus, snow peas and tiny peas instantly provide a colorful palette for the pale pasta. The vegetables in pasta dishes can be slightly undercooked to provide a crunchy texture or cooked just long enough for the different flavors to harmonize so one ingredient is not prominent.

A quick trick for cooking vegetables is to add the prepared vegetables to the hot pasta water for the last few minutes before the pasta is cooked and then drain the pasta and vegetables together.

We like to peel and seed fresh tomatoes. We peel peppers with a vegetable peeler to preserve the crispness of the raw peppers, make them easier to digest, and because it is quicker than the usual method of blistering the skin over flame and then peeling. But peeling vegetables is a personal preference. Your cooking pleasure should not be diminished by too many rules or special techniques.

In this section is a striking Confetti Pasta with red and green peppers; a wonderful Pasta with Chinese Cabbage and Black Mushrooms; a colorful vegetable curry with couscous; a hearty Pasta with Lentils, and many other different vegetable combinations. Use the freshest vegetables in season and your own favorites to create delicious new variations.

BROCCOLI AND BOWTIES

Preparation time: 30 minutes
Servings: 3 to 4

Broccoli florets team up with whimsical bowties for an attractive, nutritious luncheon or supper dish. Use broccoli stems for soup or stir-fry.

8 oz. dried bowtie shapes, or
   orecchiette pasta
1 bunch broccoli, florets only
1 tbs. full-flavored olive oil
2 large garlic cloves, minced
1/4 tsp. red pepper flakes
salt and freshly ground pepper

3 tbs. slivered sun-dried tomato
   pieces, oil packed, or 2 tbs.
   sun-dried tomato paste
1/2 cup heavy cream
1/4 cup grated Parmesan cheese
1/4 cup pine nuts, toasted

Heat pasta water. Prepare broccoli florets. Pieces should be about thumb-size in thickness. Cook pasta according to package directions. The last 5 minutes before pasta is cooked, add broccoli florets to cooking water. Heat olive oil in a large skillet. Sauté garlic and red pepper flakes 1 to 2 minutes until garlic is soft. Add cream, bring to boil and cook 2 to 3 minutes until sauce starts to thicken. Pour drained cooked pasta and broccoli into skillet. Add salt, pepper, tomato pieces and Parmesan cheese. Toss well. Top with toasted pine nuts. Serve immediately on warm plates. Pass additional Parmesan cheese.

WAGONWHEELS WITH VEGETABLES

Preparation time: 30 minutes
Servings: 4

Sliced carrots, zucchini and mushrooms repeat the wagonwheel shape for a light colorful luncheon or supper dish. This is also good with cubes of ham, cooked turkey or chicken. Serve with crisp garlic bread.

8 oz. wagonwheel pasta
1 cup carrot slices
3 small zucchini, sliced
1 lb. medium mushrooms, sliced
½ cup chopped red onion
1 garlic clove, minced
3 tbs. light olive oil

dash hot red pepper flakes
½ cup chicken stock
½ cup tomato pieces with juice
½ tsp. dried oregano or 2 tsp. fresh
1 tsp. dried sweet basil or 1 tbs. fresh
salt and freshly ground pepper
½ cup grated Parmesan cheese

Start heating pasta water in a large pot. Slice carrots, zucchini and mushrooms into ¼-inch slices. When water is boiling, add salt, wagonwheels and carrot slices. Cook pasta according to package directions.

Heat oil in a large nonstick skillet. Sauté onion and garlic over medium heat 2 to 3 minutes to soften onion. Add red pepper flakes, mushrooms and zucchini and sauté over high heat 3 to 4 minutes until mushrooms are soft. Pour in chicken stock, tomatoes with juice, oregano and sweet basil. Season with salt and pepper. Bring mixture to a boil and then simmer for about 5 minutes, or until pasta is cooked.

Drain pasta and carrots, pour into skillet with sauce and toss to combine. Pour into a warm bowl, top with cheese, and serve immediately on warm plates. Pass extra cheese.

PASTA WITH SUN-DRIED TOMATOES, MUSHROOMS AND PEAS

Preparation time: 20 minutes
Servings: 3 to 4

Sun-dried tomatoes make a terrific taste accent with fresh sweet basil, mushrooms and peas. Add a cup of diced baked ham or turkey ham for a heartier dish.

8 oz. radiatore, corkscrews or orecchiette pasta
2 tbs. light olive oil
1 small onion, chopped
8 oz. fresh mushrooms, thinly sliced
½ cup chicken stock
5 oz. frozen peas
1 tsp. cornstarch dissolved in 1 tbs. dry sherry
salt and freshly ground pepper
dash red pepper flakes
¼ cup slivered sun-dried tomatoes in oil
½ cup grated Parmesan cheese
½ cup fresh basil leaves, cut into thin strips

Bring pasta cooking water to boil in a large pot. Cook pasta while making sauce. Heat oil in a large nonstick skillet. Sauté onion 2 to 3 minutes until it softens. Turn up heat and sauté mushrooms 3 to 4 minutes. Rinse peas with cold water to defrost. Add chicken stock and peas to mushroom mixture. Simmer for 3 to 4 minutes. Stir in cornstarch mixture, salt, pepper and hot pepper flakes. Allow sauce to thicken. Add sun-dried tomato pieces. Combine hot pasta and sauce in skillet. Add Parmesan cheese and fresh basil leaves. Pour into a warm bowl and serve immediately on warm plates.

PASTA WITH LENTILS

Preparation time: 60 minutes
Servings: 3 to 4

This is a wonderful, satisfying dish for a rainy evening or when the weather turns crisp and cold. It is also delicious the second day when the flavors have had a chance to develop. Just before serving, top with a fresh peeled, seeded and chopped tomato for color and texture contrast.

¼ cup full-flavored olive oil
1 small onion diced
1 garlic clove, minced
1 cup dried lentils, picked over and rinsed
1 pkg. (10 oz.) frozen spinach, defrosted and squeezed dry
1 can (14½ oz.) chicken broth, reduced sodium
1 quart water
2 tbs. tomato paste
several generous grinds of black pepper
salt
juice of ½ a lemon
8 ozs. orecchiette
1 large or 2 small fresh tomatoes, peeled, seeded and chopped

Add olive oil to a large saucepan and heat over medium heat. When oil begins to shimmer, add onion and garlic. Reduce heat and cook until onion is translucent, but do not brown garlic. Add lentils and stir to coat with oil. Add squeezed spinach, chicken broth, water and tomato paste and bring to a boil. Reduce heat and simmer for about 40 minutes until lentils are almost done and sauce starts to thicken.

When lentils have cooked for about 25 minutes, bring pasta water to boil. Cook pasta according to package instructions. Add to simmering sauce in saucepan; season with salt, pepper and lemon juice. Pour into a warmed bowl, top with chopped tomato and serve immediately. Pass grated cheese.

NEW WORLD VEGETABLE CURRY WITH COUSCOUS

Preparation time: 40 minutes
Servings: 4

This colorful dish combines squash, eggplants, yams and corn to make a thick flavorful topping for couscous, or another pasta of your choice. Make this ahead and reheat in the microwave for a quick weekday dinner.

2 tbs. light olive oil
1 cup onion, chopped
2 garlic cloves, minced
1 small hot pepper, minced
1 tbs. curry powder
1½ cups Japanese eggplant, peeled and diced into ½-inch pieces
1½ cups yam or sweet potato, peeled and diced into ½-inch pieces

2 cups chicken stock
2 small zucchini, cut in ¼-inch slices
2 small yellow squash, cut in ¼-inch slices
kernels from 1 small ear fresh corn, optional
salt and freshly ground pepper

Heat olive oil in a large saucepan. Sauté onion, garlic and hot pepper 3 to 4 minutes until onion softens. Add curry powder; cook 1 to 2 minutes. Add eggplant and cook 2 minutes. Add yam pieces and chicken stock. Bring to a boil and simmer uncovered about 10 minutes. Stir in squashes and cook 10 minutes. Add corn, salt and pepper. Cook for 5 minutes. Cook couscous. Serve in shallow bowls. Place a large scoop of couscous in the bowl and top with about 1 cup of curry sauce.

Couscous

1½ cups water
2 tbs. vegetable oil

1 cup couscous
salt

Heat water and oil to boiling in a large nonstick skillet. Add couscous and salt, cover, remove from heat and allow to stand for 5 minutes. Uncover and fluff grains with a fork.

PASTA WITH CHINESE CABBAGE AND BLACK MUSHROOMS

Preparation time: 30 minutes
Servings: 3 to 4

This full-flavored pasta dish features all the wonderful flavors of Chinese food. Dried black mushrooms are softened, slivered, and sautéed with fresh mushrooms, crisp Napa cabbage and onions. Use fusilli or gemellini-shaped pasta.

8 oz. dried fusilli or gemellini
8 small dried black mushrooms
6-7 cups Napa cabbage, thinly sliced into ¼-inch slivers
3 tbs. vegetable oil
2 tsp. minced fresh ginger root
8 ozs. fresh mushrooms, thinly sliced
1 medium onion, thinly sliced
red pepper flakes
2 tbs. soy sauce
1½ cups beef broth
2 tbs. sesame oil
2 tbs. cornstarch dissolved in 3 tbs. water

Cover dried mushrooms with boiling water and let stand about 20 minutes. Squeeze dry and cut out tough center stem. Cut in thin slivers. Bring pasta water to a boil. Prepare cabbage; slice fresh mushrooms and onion.

Heat vegetable oil in a large sauté pan. Sauté minced ginger 1 minute. Add onion and fresh mushrooms. Sauté 3 to 4 minutes over high heat. Add dried slivered mushrooms, red pepper flakes, soy sauce and beef broth; bring to a boil. Simmer about 5 minutes. Add cabbage and cook 1 to 2 minutes until cabbage softens. Stir in a little dissolved cornstarch to thicken sauce, using just enough to make a glazing but not thick sauce. Add drained, cooked pasta to skillet and toss. Pour into a warm serving bowl. Serve immediately.

PASTA WITH FENNEL AND ROASTED RED PEPPERS

Preparation time: 30 minutes
Servings: 3 to 4

Anise-flavored fennel strips cook with the pasta and are tossed with roasted red pepper pieces and grated Gruyére cheese. Garnish pasta with some of the fine fennel greens.

8 oz. dried penne
2 medium sized fennel bulbs
2 tbs. butter
½ cup onion, chopped
2 cloves garlic, minced
¼ tsp. hot pepper flakes
3 tbs. heavy cream
½ cup roasted red pepper or pimento strips
¾ cup coarsely grated Gruyére cheese
salt and freshly ground pepper
fennel greens and grated Parmesan cheese for garnish

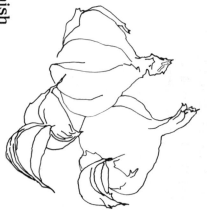

Heat pasta water. Cut fennel tops off at top of bulb. Discard any tough or damaged outer fennel bulb. Cut into ¼-inch vertical slices. Cut slices into 3 or 4 strips. Add fennel strips to boiling pasta after pasta has cooked 2 minutes.

Heat butter in a large nonstick skillet. Sauté onions and garlic over medium heat 3 to 4 minutes until onions have softened. Add hot pepper flakes, cream and roasted peppers. Cook over low heat 2 to 3 minutes to blend flavors.

When pasta is done, drain and pour into a warm serving bowl. Add onion, red pepper mixture, Gruyére, salt and pepper. Toss to combine. Serve immediately on warm plates. Garnish with finely chopped fennel greens and pass Parmesan cheese.

PASTA WITH SUGAR SNAPS AND SNOW PEAS

Preparation time: 30 minutes
Servings: 3 to 4

Crisp green sugar snaps and snow peas are paired with dried black mushrooms for a tasty pasta dish.

4-5 dried black mushrooms, softened in boiling water for 20 min.
8 oz. dried fusilli, gemellini or penne-shaped pasta
4 oz. sugar snap peas, stemmed
4 oz. snow peas, stemmed and cut into ½-inch strips
2 tbs. light olive or vegetable oil
4-6 green onions, thinly sliced
1 cup chicken stock
¼ cup dry sherry
1 tsp. cornstarch dissolved in 1 tbs. water
1 tsp. sesame oil
salt and freshly ground pepper
1 medium tomato, peeled, seeded, chopped
grated Parmesan cheese

Drain and squeeze softened mushrooms very dry. Cut out tough center stem and cut into very thin strips. Bring pasta water to a boil. One minute before pasta has finished cooking, add sugar snap peas to water.

In a large nonstick skillet, sauté onions in oil 2 to 3 minutes to soften. Add chicken stock and sherry, bring to a boil and cook 2 to 3 minutes. Add sesame oil, salt and pepper. Pour drained pasta and peas into skillet and toss to combine. Bring sauce to a boil. If very thin, thicken with some dissolved cornstarch so sauce is thick enough to coat pasta lightly. Pour into a warm serving bowl, top with chopped tomato, and serve immediately on warm plates. Pass Parmesan cheese, if desired.

CONFETTI PASTA

Preparation time: 30 minutes
Servings: 4

Fresh red and green peppers make this a colorful pasta dish. Peeling the fresh peppers with a vegetable peeler results in a crisp, crunchy texture very different from roasted peppers, and is worth the effort.

12 oz. fresh pasta or 8 oz. dried pasta
1 fresh red pepper
1 fresh green pepper
2 tbs. olive oil
1 small onion, chopped
2 garlic cloves, minced
½ cup petite green peas, defrosted
¼ cup sliced ripe olives

½ tsp. dried oregano
½ tsp. dried sweet basil
3 tbs. chopped fresh parsley
1 cup cubed (¼-inch) fontina or other mild cheese
freshly ground black pepper
salt to taste
2 tbs. butter, melted, optional

Start heating pasta cooking water in a large pot. Cut peppers into vertical sections following the natural ridges. Remove seeds and membrane. Using a vegetable peeler, remove thin outer skin. Cut into ¼-inch squares or julienne. Begin cooking pasta. Heat olive oil in a medium-sized skillet. Sauté onion and garlic until soft but not brown. Add peppers. Cook 1 minute. Stir in green peas, olives, oregano, basil, parsley, cheese, salt and pepper; remove from heat. Toss cooked, well-drained pasta with melted butter if desired. Add approximately one-half of the sauce, tossing with two forks. Top with remaining sauce and serve immediately on warm plates.

Variation: Add 1 cup diced ham or slivered smoked turkey breast.

Wine suggestion: Dry Riesling

PASTA PRIMAVERA

Preparation time: 30 minutes
Servings: 3 to 4

With lots of fresh vegetables, this Italian classic is as healthful as it is delicious.

12 oz. fresh or 8 oz. dried tagliarini, spaghetti or fettuccine
2 medium tomatoes, peeled, seeded and coarsely chopped
4 tbs. olive oil
1 small onion, finely chopped
1/4 tsp. red pepper flakes
1/2 lb. mushrooms, thinly sliced
1 garlic clove, minced
1 cup diagonally sliced asparagus or green beans
1 cup cauliflower florets
1 medium yellow squash, thinly sliced
1 medium red or green pepper, peeled and cut into thin strips
1 cup coarsely grated carrots
1/2 cup fresh blanched or frozen peas
salt and pepper
3 tbs. finely chopped parsley
1/3 cup Parmesan cheese

Start heating pasta cooking water in a large pot. Time pasta so it is cooked when sauce is finished. Heat olive oil in a large skillet. Sauté onion and red pepper flakes for 3 to 4 minutes. Add mushrooms and garlic. Cook for 2 minutes over medium-high heat. Add asparagus, cauliflower, yellow squash and peppers. Cover and cook 2 minutes. Add carrots, tomato pieces, peas, salt and pepper. Cook 2 to 3 minutes. Toss with hot, well-drained pasta. Top with parsley and Parmesan cheese. Serve immediately on warm plates.

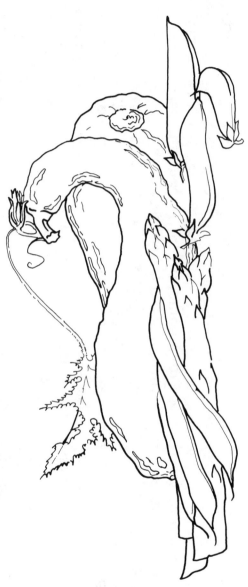

EAST MEETS WEST PASTA

Preparation time: 30 minutes
Servings: 3 to 4

Fresh snow peas and bean sprouts along with other garden vegetables make this a colorful and delicious main course.

12 oz. fresh or 8 oz. dried tagliarini
   or fettuccine
¼ cup olive oil
1 small onion, finely chopped
½ tsp. red pepper flakes, or to taste
½ lb. fresh mushrooms, thinly sliced
2 garlic cloves, minced

1 cup thinly sliced yellow squash
1 cup thinly sliced zucchini
1 cup snow peas, strings removed
1 cup fresh bean sprouts
1 cup chopped tomatoes
¾ cup heavy cream
salt and pepper to taste

Bring pasta cooking water to a boil in a large pot. Cook pasta while making sauce. Heat oil in a large skillet. Sauté chopped onion with red pepper flakes 3 to 4 minutes. Add mushrooms and garlic. Sauté 2 minutes. Add yellow squash, zucchini, snow peas, bean sprouts, tomato pieces, cream, salt and pepper. Cook over high heat 2 to 3 minutes until cream starts to thicken and vegetables are crisp-tender. Drain pasta well. Combine approximately ½ of the sauce with hot pasta. Top with remaining vegetables and sauce. Serve on warm plates. Pass freshly grated Parmesan cheese.

SPINACH AND MUSHROOM PASTA

Preparation time: 15 minutes
Servings: 3 to 4

Puree cooked spinach and cottage cheese in a blender or food processor to make a lovely green pasta sauce.

12 oz. fresh pasta or 8 oz. dried spaghetti or linguine
2 tbs. butter
8 oz. fresh mushrooms, thinly sliced
5 to 6 green onions, thinly sliced

1 cup cooked spinach, well drained
1 cup small curd cottage cheese
1/4 cup heavy cream
salt and white pepper to taste
grated Parmesan cheese for garnish

Start heating pasta cooking water in a large pot. Melt butter in a medium-sized skillet. When foaming, add mushrooms and sauté 2 to 3 minutes. Add green onions and cook for another minute. Place cooked, well-drained spinach, cottage cheese and heavy cream in a blender container or food processor bowl. Process until smooth. Add to mushrooms and onions; season with salt and pepper. Start pasta cooking. Just before pasta is done, heat mushroom and spinach mixture. Combine with hot, well-drained pasta. Serve immediately on warm plates. Pass freshly grated Parmesan cheese.

PASTA WITH FRESH ZUCCHINI

Preparation time: 30 minutes
Servings: 3 to 4

Here is a flavorful crisp zucchini and tomato topping for pasta.

12 oz. fresh pasta or 8 oz. dried pasta
2 tbs. olive oil
1 medium onion, chopped
1 garlic clove, minced
3 medium zucchini
1 can (15 oz.) tomato sauce

½ tsp. dried marjoram
½ tsp. dried oregano
½ tsp. dried sweet basil
½ tsp. salt
¼ tsp. white pepper

Start heating pasta cooking water in a large pot. Time pasta so it is cooked when sauce is ready. Heat oil in a medium saucepan. Sauté onion until soft but not brown. Add garlic. Slice zucchini in half lengthwise, and then slice across in ¼- to ½-inch slices. Add to onion and garlic. Stir in tomato sauce, marjoram, oregano, sweet basil, salt and pepper. Cover and simmer 15 minutes, stirring occasionally. Mix with hot, well-drained pasta. Pass freshly grated Parmesan cheese.

FETTUCCINE WITH BROCCOLI AND CARROTS

Preparation time: 30 minutes
Servings: 4 to 5

Crisp vegetables add interest to this quick and colorful pasta dish. Try it with zucchini instead of broccoli.

12 oz. fresh or 8 oz. dried fettuccine
4 medium carrots
3 cups broccoli pieces
5 green onions

4-5 strips bacon or pancetta, optional
2 tbs. olive oil
2 large garlic cloves, minced
1 tbs. red wine vinegar

Start heating pasta cooking water in a large pot. Cut carrots into matchsticks approximately 1½ inches long. Cut broccoli florets from stems and slice stems into paper-thin pieces. Thinly slice green onions. Sauté bacon in a large skillet until crisp. Remove from pan and crumble into small pieces. Begin cooking pasta. Pour out all but 2 tbs. bacon drippings. Add olive oil to bacon drippings. When oil is hot, add carrots, broccoli, green onions and garlic. Toss to coat vegetables with oil. Cover and cook for 1 to 2 minutes. Add vinegar and cook for another minute. Place cooked, well-drained pasta in a large warm bowl. Add vegetable mixture and toss to combine ingredients. Serve on warm plates.

PASTA WITH FRESH VEGETABLES   101

PASTA PROVENÇAL

Preparation time: 15 minutes
Servings: 3 to 4

Crisp eggplant and red pepper slivers make a quick, savory first course or luncheon dish.

12 oz. fresh pasta or 8 oz. dried spaghetti
2 Japanese eggplants or 1 small eggplant
1/4 cup olive oil

1 red pepper, peeled and julienned
3 garlic cloves, minced
salt and pepper to taste
2 tbs. chopped parsley
grated Parmesan cheese

Start heating pasta cooking water in a large pot. Time pasta so it is cooked when sauce is ready. Cut unpeeled eggplant into 1/4-inch slices, and then into 1/2-inch pieces. Lightly dust eggplant pieces with flour. Heat oil in a large skillet. When oil shimmers, add eggplant pieces and sauté over medium heat for approximately 2 minutes until lightly browned on one side. Turn eggplant pieces over. Add red pepper slivers, garlic, salt and pepper. Sauté for approximately 2 to 3 minutes until eggplant is crisp and lightly browned. Toss with hot, well-drained pasta. Top with parsley and serve immediately on warm plates. Pass freshly grated Parmesan cheese.

PASTA WITH SEAFOOD

Seafood and pasta are another natural alliance. There may be as many different kinds of seafood available as there are pasta shapes.

Always choose the freshest seafood available because anything less will detract from the dish. It is important not to cook fish or shellfish too long. Seafood needs cooking only to firm its flesh. To avoid overcooking, most of the following recipes call for adding the fish or shellfish when the sauce is almost done, or sautéing it separately and then combining it with the pasta just before serving.

PASTA WITH ASPARAGUS AND SHRIMP

Preparation time: 45 minutes
Servings: 3 to 4

Use penne-shaped pasta and cut the asparagus in diagonal slices to match the penne in shape. A quick way to blanch the asparagus is to add it to the hot cooking water for the last 2 minutes before the pasta is done, and then drain the pasta and asparagus at the same time.

8 oz. dried penne pasta
2 cups asparagus (8 oz. trimmed)
1 tbs. light-flavored olive oil
6 green onions, thinly sliced
¾ lb. small shrimp, uncooked, shelled and deveined
¼ cup plain yogurt
¼ cup heavy cream
salt and freshly ground pepper
¼ tsp. dried tarragon
1 tbs. lemon juice
2 tbs. parsley, finely chopped

Start heating pasta water in a large pot. Cut trimmed asparagus into thin diagonal slices and set aside. Heat olive oil in a large nonstick skillet. Sauté onions over low heat 1 to 2 minutes until translucent. Add shrimp and cook over medium heat until they start to turn pink. Add yogurt, cream, salt, pepper, tarragon and lemon juice. Cook for another 1 to 2 minutes until mixture is hot, but not boiling. Meanwhile, when water is boiling, salt water, add pasta and cook according to package directions. Two minutes before pasta is done, add asparagus slices to cooking water. When pasta is done, drain and pour pasta and asparagus into the skillet with the sauce. Combine pasta, asparagus and sauce, add parsley and pour into a warm serving bowl. Serve immediately on warm plates.

RIGATONI WITH ZESTY TUNA SAUCE

Preparation time: 40 minutes
Servings: 3 to 4

Fresh tuna pieces simmered in a hearty tomato sauce make a satisfying dinner. Serve with a fresh green salad and some crisp garlic bread.

8 oz. dried rigatoni, ziti, penne
   or mostaccioli
3 tbs. full-flavored olive oil
½ cup onion, chopped
2 garlic cloves, minced
dash red pepper flakes
1 can (16 oz.) tomato pieces
   with sauce
2 tbs. tomato paste or sun-dried
   tomato paste

2 anchovy filets, rinsed, dried, chopped
¼ cup dry white wine
½ cup kalamata olives, pitted,
   coarsely chopped
1 tbs. balsamic or red wine vinegar
1 lb. fresh tuna, cut into 1-inch
   pieces
salt and freshly ground pepper
grated Parmesan or asiago cheese
Italian parsley, chopped, for garnish

Heat olive oil in a large skillet. Sauté onion 3 to 4 minutes until softened. Add garlic, red pepper flakes, tomato pieces and tomato paste. Cook 3 to 4 minutes until juices thicken slightly. Add anchovy pieces, olives, balsamic vinegar, tuna pieces, salt and pepper. Simmer 3 to 4 minutes until tuna pieces are cooked through. Add hot drained pasta to skillet. Toss and pour into a warm bowl. Serve immediately on warmed plates. Garnish with parsley. Pass Parmesan or asiago cheese.

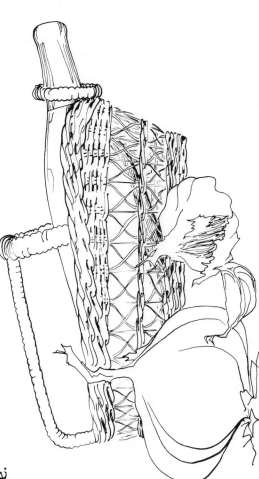

PASTA WITH SALMON
AND SPRING VEGETABLES

Preparation time: 30 minutes
Servings: 3 to 4

Colorful vegetables and chunks of fresh pink salmon make a delicious main course. Time the pasta cooking so you have about 4 minutes to cook the vegetables and salmon pieces before the pasta is done.

8 oz. dried corkscrews or radiatore

2 tbs. butter

3 tbs. finely chopped shallots

1 cup clam juice

1 tbs. lemon juice

½ cup heavy cream

2 small carrots, thinly sliced in rounds

1 small zucchini, thinly sliced in rounds

2 tbs. fresh dill or 1 tbs. fresh thyme leaves, or ½ tsp. dried herbs

salt and freshly ground pepper

1 lb. fresh salmon, cut into 1-inch pieces

½ cup frozen peas, rinsed with cold water

2 small Italian plum tomatoes, seeded and chopped

Heat pasta water. Cook pasta according to package directions. Melt butter in a large skillet and sauté shallots 1 to 2 minutes. Add clam juice and lemon juice. Turn heat on high and reduce volume by about half. Add cream, lower heat, and simmer 2 to 3 minutes. About 4 minutes before pasta is done, add carrots, zucchini, dill, salt and pepper to cream mixture. Cook over medium heat about 2 minutes. Add salmon pieces and peas. Cook 1 to 2 minutes, turning salmon pieces so they cook evenly. Add tomato pieces. Pour cooked pasta into a large warm serving bowl. Pour sauce over pasta and toss gently so salmon pieces stay intact. Serve immediately.

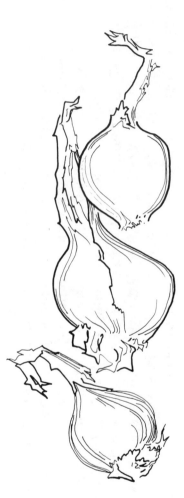

PASTA WITH SCALLOPS AND RED PEPPERS

Preparation time: 30 minutes
Servings: 3 to 4

Red peppers are a pleasant contrast to pasta and scallops in flavor as well as visually.

12 oz. fresh pasta or 8 oz. dried pasta	¼ tsp. white pepper
2 medium-sized red bell peppers	1 lb. scallops, cut in half if large size
2 tbs. butter	salt
3 tbs. minced shallots	2 tbs. minced parsley
1 cup cream	

This is a very fast sauce, so time pasta to be done approximately 6 minutes after you start the sauce. Cut red peppers along ridges and remove membrane and seeds. Using a swivel blade vegetable peeler, remove outer skin from pepper sections. Cut in thin slivers or julienne. Melt butter in a medium skillet. Sauté shallots 1 minute. Add cream and white pepper. Turn heat on high and reduce cream 2 to 3 minutes until it starts to thicken. Reduce heat to medium. Add scallops and salt. Cook 1 minute. Add red peppers and cook 1 minute. Toss hot, well-drained pasta with about half of the scallop mixture. Top with remaining scallops and parsley. Serve on warm plates.

PASTA WITH SCALLOPS AND WALNUTS

Preparation time: 30 minutes
Servings: 3 to 4

*For a pretty contrast with the scallops, use thin green pasta or **Spicy Red Pepper Pasta**, page 20.*

12 oz. fresh pasta or 8 oz. dried pasta
¼ cup chopped walnuts or toasted
  bread crumbs
1 lb. bay scallops
4 tbs. butter

2 garlic cloves, minced
red pepper flakes to taste
grated rind from ½ lemon
1 tbs. lemon juice
2 tbs. minced parsley

Cook pasta while preparing sauce. Drain well. Toast walnuts in a 300° oven for 5 or 6 minutes until they are slightly browned. Set aside. Melt butter in a large skillet. Sauté scallops, garlic and red pepper flakes for approximately 2 minutes. Add lemon rind and juice. Add cooked, well-drained pasta to skillet. Add walnuts and parsley; toss until mixed. Serve immediately on warm plates.

Wine suggestion: Chardonnay or Pinot Blanc

PASTA WITH SHRIMP
AND DILL SAUCE

Preparation time: 15 minutes
Servings: 3 to 4

This delicate sauce is lightly flavored with dill. Use fettuccine or wider egg noodles for the pasta.

12 oz. fresh pasta or 8 oz. dried pasta
¾ cup plain yogurt
¼ cup heavy cream
1 tbs. soy sauce
1 tsp. Worcestershire sauce
½ tsp. dry mustard
½ tsp. dried dill weed or 1 tbs. finely chopped fresh dill
¼ tsp. white pepper
½ lb. small cooked shrimp

Cook pasta while you are making the sauce. Drain well. Gently heat yogurt, cream, soy sauce, Worcestershire, dry mustard, dill and pepper. Do not allow to boil. Add shrimp and heat to serving temperature. Toss with hot well-drained pasta and serve immediately on warm plates.

Wine suggestion: Chardonnay or Sauvignon Blanc

PASTA WITH CRAB

Preparation time: 15 minutes
Servings: 3 to 4

*Use green fettuccine or **Spicy Red Pepper Pasta**, page 20, for this quick and pretty seafood pasta.*

12 oz. fresh pasta or 8 oz. dried pasta
3 tbs. butter
2 tbs. minced shallots
6 to 8 fresh mushrooms, sliced
1/2 tsp. grated fresh ginger
1/2 cup half and half

3 oz. cream cheese, cut in small cubes
1 1/2 cups flaked crab meat
dash cayenne pepper
salt and pepper to taste
2 tbs. minced parsley

Have pasta cooking water hot and time the pasta to be done when sauce is ready. Drain well. Melt butter in a medium skillet. When foaming add shallots, mushrooms and fresh ginger. Sauté 3 to 4 minutes until mushrooms are done. Add half and half and cream cheese. Increase heat and cook 2 to 3 minutes until sauce starts to thicken. Add crab meat, cayenne, salt and pepper. Cook only until crab is hot, stirring as little as possible. Toss hot, well-drained pasta with sauce and serve immediately on warm plates.

Wine suggestion: Pinot Blanc or Dry Semillon

CURRIED PASTA WITH MUSSELS

Preparation time: 30 minutes
Servings: 3 to 4

The light curry flavor is delightful with both the pasta and the mussels. Clams are also delicious in this dish.

12 oz. fresh or 8 oz. dried linguine
3 to 4 dozen mussels
5 tbs. olive oil
¼ tsp. dried hot red pepper flakes
½ cup dry white wine or vermouth
¼ cup heavy cream
1 large onion, thinly sliced
1 large garlic clove, minced
1½ tsp. curry powder
1 cup fresh tomato pieces
salt and pepper to taste
⅓ cup chopped roasted peanuts

Have pasta cooking water hot and time pasta to be done when the sauce is ready. Scrub mussels with a stiff brush and remove beards. Wash well. Heat 2 tbs. olive oil in a large skillet or heavy pot. Add pepper flakes and sauté for 1 minute. Add mussels and wine. Cover pot and cook over high heat 3 to 4 minutes, or until shells have all opened. Shake pan occasionally while mussels are steaming. Remove from heat and let cool. When cool enough to handle, remove mussels from shells. Reserve 1 to 2 shells for garnishing individual plates or a few for a large serving bowl. Strain ¾ cup mussel liquid through cheesecloth into a measuring cup. Add ¼ cup heavy cream.

Heat 3 tbs. olive oil in a large skillet. Add onion slices and cook until onion is soft and translucent, but not browned. Add garlic and curry powder to onion. Cook 2 minutes. Add tomato pieces, cream-mussel juice mixture, salt and pepper. Cook over high heat 3 to 4 minutes until cream starts to thicken. Add mussels to sauce and just heat through. Mix ½ of the sauce with hot, well-drained pasta. Top with remaining sauce and chopped peanuts. Garnish with reserved mussel shells. Serve immediately.

Wine suggestion: Chenin Blanc or Riesling

PASTA WITH FISH
VERA CRUZ STYLE

Preparation time: 30 minutes
Servings: 4 to 5

The hearty flavors of tomato and red pepper complement sea bass, rock cod or other firm-fleshed fish. Serve in shallow soup plates with crusty French bread to finish off the sauce.

12 oz. fresh pasta or 8 oz. dried pasta (shells or bowties)
1 can (28 oz.) Italian-style tomatoes
1 large red pepper, peeled, seeded and chopped
2 tbs. olive oil
1 small onion, finely chopped
1 large garlic clove, minced
1 tbs. anchovy paste
½ tsp. red pepper flakes or small fresh hot pepper, diced
1 lb. sea bass or rock cod
grated rind and juice from 1 small orange
1 tbs. lemon juice
salt and pepper
grated Parmesan cheese

Have pasta cooking water hot and time pasta to be done when sauce is ready. Drain tomatoes in a sieve. Reserve juice and discard seeds. Cut out hard core of tomato and chop coarsely. Peel, seed and chop pepper. Heat olive oil in a heavy saucepan. Add onion and cook 3 to 4 minutes until soft but not brown. Add pepper, garlic, anchovy paste and red pepper flakes. Cook over low heat for 2 minutes. Add reserved tomato juice. Reduce over high heat to approximately 1/2 of original volume. Cut fish into 1-inch squares. Add fish, lemon juice, orange rind, orange juice and tomatoes to saucepan. Simmer gently 2 to 3 minutes until fish is just done. Do not overcook. Add cooked, well-drained pasta to sauce and toss to combine. Serve immediately in shallow soup plates. Pass freshly grated cheese.

Wine suggestion: well chilled white jug wine

SHRIMP CHOW MEIN

Preparation time: 30 minutes
Servings: 2 to 3

This classic Chinese dish goes together very quickly after the shrimp are prepared and the vegetables sliced.

6 oz. fresh Chinese noodles or 4 oz. dried noodles or spaghettini

2 tsp. cornstarch

1 tbs. plus 1 tsp. soy sauce

1 egg white

1/4 tsp. white pepper

6 oz. small raw shrimp, peeled, deveined, and cut in half lengthwise

6 tbs. vegetable oil

1 large garlic clove, peeled and flattened

1/4-inch slice fresh ginger root

3 green onions, white part only, thinly sliced

6 oz. small mushrooms, thinly sliced

6 oz. fresh bean sprouts or thinly sliced raw cabbage

1 tsp. sesame oil

Cook noodles and drain well. Combine cornstarch, 1 tsp. soy sauce, egg white and white pepper. Pour over shrimp. Mix well and set aside. Add 2 tbs. oil to wok or large nonstick frying pan. Add garlic and ginger. Cook over high heat until slightly brown. Remove garlic and ginger; discard. Add cooked noodles to frying pan. Stir to coat with oil and allow to lightly brown on all sides. Turn out onto a plate covered with paper towels. Add 2 tbs. more oil to frying pan. When hot, add shrimp mixture. Stir quickly for 1 to 2 minutes until shrimp are opaque and firm. Turn out onto another plate covered with paper towels.

Add remaining 2 tbs. vegetable oil to frying pan. When hot, add onion and mushrooms and stir for 1 to 2 minutes. Add bean sprouts and toss quickly. Return shrimp and cooked noodles to frying pan and toss. Remove from heat and sprinkle with remaining 1 tbs. soy sauce and sesame oil. Stir quickly and serve immediately on warm plates.

Variation: Uncooked chicken cut into 1/2-inch cubes can be substituted for the shrimp.

Wine suggestion: Chenin Blanc or Riesling

BAY SCALLOPS WITH ANGEL HAIR PASTA

Preparation time: 20 minutes
Servings: 2 dinner or
4 appetizer

Tender strands of pasta accented with lemon, delicate bay scallops, and fresh sweet basil make an elegant first course or dinner for two.

½ lbs. bay scallops
4 oz. dried angel hair or capellini-
  shaped pasta
1 tbs. butter
3-4 green onions, thinly sliced
grated zest from 1 lemon

2 tbs. lemon juice
3 tbs. heavy cream
salt and white pepper
2 tbs. fresh sweet basil, slivered or
2 tbs. Italian parsley, chopped

Wash scallops and remove tiny, tough muscle on side of scallop. Bring pasta water to a boil. Melt butter in a medium nonstick skillet. Sauté onions 1 to 2 minutes, just to soften. Add scallops and cook 1 to 2 minutes. Stir in lemon zest and juice. Let stand until pasta is cooked. Just before pasta is done, add cream, salt and pepper to skillet. Bring to a boil. Add drained hot pasta to skillet and toss to combine. Serve immediately on warm plates. Garnish with slivered fresh basil.

PASTA WITH WHITE CLAM SAUCE

Preparation time: 15 minutes
Servings: 4 to 5

Clams cooked with white wine and garlic make a delicious quick pasta sauce.

1 lb. fresh linguine or 12 oz. dried
  linguine
1/4 cup butter
1 to 2 large garlic cloves, minced
2 tbs. flour
2 cans (6½ oz. each) chopped clams

1/4 cup dry white wine or dry vermouth
half and half
1/4 cup finely chopped parsley
1/2 tsp. dried thyme
salt and pepper to taste

Heat pasta cooking water in a large pot. Melt butter in a small saucepan. Add garlic to butter and cook 1 minute. Stir in flour and cook 2 minutes. Drain clams, reserving juice, Combine reserved clam juice and white wine. Add enough half and half to make 2 cups liquid. Add to flour mixture gradually and cook until sauce thickens slightly. Add parsley, thyme, salt and pepper. Simmer for approximately 10 minutes. Cook pasta while sauce is simmering. Add clams to sauce and heat to serving temperature. Combine with hot, well-drained pasta and serve immediately on warm plates.

Wine suggestion: Sauvignon Blanc or Chardonnay

PASTA WITH POULTRY AND MEAT

Pasta pairs well with all kinds of poultry and meat, and there is no limit to savory combinations. Substitute turkey tenderloins or fillets for lower fat, delicious eating. The deli style turkey hams, smoked turkey sausages and meats provide a lot of hearty flavor.

We have included one tomato-based sauce with sausage. Bolognese and marinara style sauces are not included in this edition because they have long simmering times, and because there are so many good prepared ones available.

Consider substituting different shapes of pasta for rice or potatoes in your favorite casseroles for a new look and taste.

PUNJAB-STYLE CHICKEN AND MACARONI

Preparation time: 30 minutes
Baking time: 20 minutes
Servings: 4

The blending of delicious spices makes this pasta dish one of our favorites.

1½ cups macaroni or tubetti
4 chicken breast halves
3 to 4 tbs. butter
¼ cup minced green onions
1 garlic clove, minced
2 tbs. flour
1¾ cups chicken broth
1 cup sour cream

¼ tsp. **each** cinnamon, coriander, ginger, pepper and cumin seed
½ tsp. ground cardamom
½ tsp. salt
1 tsp. soy sauce
¼ tsp. Tabasco, or to taste
grated lemon rind
3 tbs. toasted sesame seeds

Cook pasta as directed on package. Skin and bone chicken. Melt butter in a medium skillet. Sauté chicken breasts over medium heat 3 to 4 minutes each side. Remove from skillet and set aside. Add green onions and garlic to pan. Cook 1 to 2 minutes. Stir in flour and cook 1 minute. Add chicken broth. Cook, stirring, until sauce thickens. Add sour cream, cinnamon, coriander, ginger, pepper, cumin, cardamom, salt, soy sauce, Tabasco and lemon rind. Mix well. Place well-drained pasta in a buttered casserole. Cover with chicken breasts, topped with sour cream sauce and sesame seeds. Bake in a 350° oven 15 to 20 minutes.

CHICKEN WITH ITALIAN SAUSAGES AND PASTA

Preparation time: 30 minutes
Servings: 3 to 4

Tender nuggets of chicken and mild Italian sausages make a delicious hearty pasta main course.

8 oz. dried pasta (small bowties or fettuccine)
3 mild or hot Italian sausages
¼ cup dry white wine or water
3 chicken breast halves, skinned and boned
flour, salt and pepper to coat chicken
2 tbs. butter
3 tbs. minced shallots
1 cup chicken broth
½ cup tomatoes, peeled, seeded and chopped
2 to 3 tbs. coarsely chopped pimiento
salt and pepper
2 tbs. minced parsley

Place sausages and white wine in a small saucepan. Cover and bring to a boil. Simmer 5 minutes. Uncover and prick sausages to release fat. Increase heat to evaporate liquid and lightly brown sausages. When sausages cool, cut into 1/2-inch rounds. Cut chicken breasts into 1-inch squares. Dust lightly with seasoned flour.

Melt butter in a medium skillet over medium heat. When foaming, add chicken and sauté until lightly browned, about 2 minutes on each side. Remove from pan. Reduce heat to low and add shallots. Stir for 1 minute. Add chicken broth and stir to remove browned bits from bottom of pan. Bring to a boil. Add chicken pieces, sausages, chopped tomato, pimiento, salt and pepper. Stir for 1 minute to heat through. Place hot, drained pasta in a large heated bowl. Add sauce and toss to combine. Sprinkle with parsley. Serve immediately on warm plates.

Wine suggestion: Chardonnay or Cabernet Blanc

JUMBO SHELLS
STUFFED WITH CHICKEN

Preparation time: 30 minutes
Cooking time: 20 to 25 minutes
Servings: 4

Use leftover chicken or turkey in this delicious first course or luncheon entrée.

8 oz. jumbo shells
Chicken Nut Filling, below

Gruyére and Sherry Sauce, page 127
grated Parmesan cheese

Cook shells as directed. Drain and rinse with cold water. Prepare filling and sauce as directed. Stuff shells with filling mixture using a small spoon. Place stuffed shells in buttered individual ramekins or a large casserole. Top with sauce. Sprinkle with Parmesan cheese. Bake in a 350° oven until heated through and bubbly. Place under broiler to brown lightly. Serve immediately.

Chicken Nut Filling

1½ cups diced cooked chicken
½ cup coarsely chopped pecans
4 tbs. finely chopped parsley
1 egg

1 cup ricotta cheese
3 tbs. Parmesan cheese
salt and white pepper

Mix ingredients together well. Stuff cooked shells with mixture.

Gruyére and Sherry Sauce

2 tbs. butter
1/4 cup minced shallots
3 tbs. flour
1 1/4 cups chicken broth
1/4 cup dry sherry
salt and white pepper
1/2 cup grated Gruyére cheese or Swiss cheese
1/4 cup heavy cream

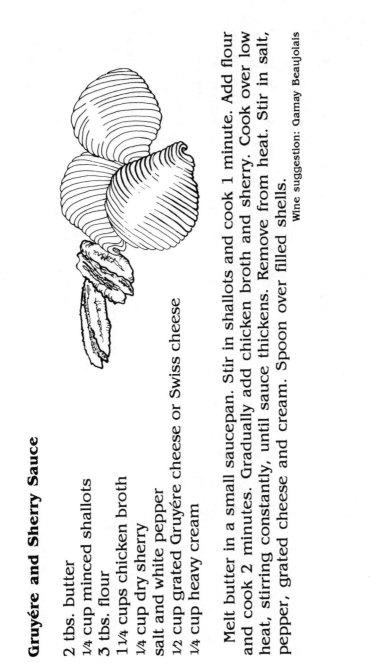

Melt butter in a small saucepan. Stir in shallots and cook 1 minute. Add flour and cook 2 minutes. Gradually add chicken broth and sherry. Cook over low heat, stirring constantly, until sauce thickens. Remove from heat. Stir in salt, pepper, grated cheese and cream. Spoon over filled shells.

Wine suggestion: Gamay Beaujolais

SHELLS WITH BROCCOLI AND CANADIAN BACON

Preparation time: 30 minutes
Baking time: 15 minutes
Servings: 4

Stuffed shells arranged in an oven-to-table serving dish make an attractive buffet or potluck main course.

8 manicotti shells
Cheese Sauce, page 129
1 tbs. butter
4 green onions, thinly sliced
1 cup diced Canadian bacon or cooked ham
1 cup ricotta cheese
4 tbs. grated Parmesan cheese
1 egg
salt and pepper
2 cups coarsely chopped cooked broccoli

Cook pasta shells in boiling water according to package directions. Drain and rinse in cold water for easier handling. Drain again. Prepare cheese sauce as directed. Melt butter in a small skillet. Sauté onions for 1 to 2 minutes to soften. Add Canadian bacon pieces and cook for 1 to 2 minutes. In a small bowl, combine ricotta, Parmesan cheese, egg, salt and pepper. Mix well. Add bacon mixture, chopped broccoli and ½ cup cheese sauce. Use a teaspoon to stuff shells with filling. Place stuffed shells in a buttered oven-proof baking dish or individual au gratin dishes. Spoon remaining cheese sauce over shells. Bake in a 350° oven 15 minutes until hot and bubbly. Place under broiler to brown lightly.

Cheese Sauce

3 tbs. butter
3 tbs. flour
2 cups milk

1½ tsp. Worcestershire sauce
¾ cup grated Swiss cheese
salt and pepper

Melt butter in a small saucepan. Add flour and cook, stirring, for 2 minutes. Gradually add milk and Worcestershire sauce. Cook, stirring constantly, until sauce thickens. Add cheese, salt and pepper. Stir to blend. Use as directed.

SPICY PORK WITH NOODLES

Preparation time: 30 minutes
Servings: 6

This is a zesty stir-fry dish. Chicken or shrimp can be substituted for pork.

1 lb. Chinese noodles
1 pkg. (10 oz.) frozen peas
1½ lbs. pork tenderloin
1½ tbs. cornstarch
2 tbs. soy sauce
2 tbs. dry sherry
7 tbs. vegetable oil
1 lb. fresh mushrooms, sliced
1 garlic clove, minced
6 green onions, thinly sliced
1 green pepper, coarsely chopped
½ tsp. dried red pepper flakes, or to taste
2 cups chicken broth
1 tsp. sesame oil

Cook noodles according to package directions. Drain and set aside. Rinse frozen peas with cold water to defrost and set aside. Slice pork into 1/4-inch x 1-inch matchsticks. Combine sliced pork with cornstarch, soy sauce and sherry. Let stand 10 to 15 minutes.

Heat 4 tbs. oil in a large frying pan or wok. Sauté mushrooms 4 to 5 minutes. Remove from frying pan and set aside. Heat 3 tbs. oil in same frying pan or wok. When very hot, add marinated pork, green onions, green pepper, garlic and red pepper flakes. Stir constantly 3 to 4 minutes until pork is cooked.

Remove mixture from frying pan and pour off any remaining oil. Stir in chicken broth. Bring to a boil. Scrape brown bits from bottom of pan. Add mushrooms, pork mixture, sesame oil, peas and cooked noodles. Cook, stirring, a few minutes until all ingredients are hot. Serve in a large warm bowl.

TURKEY, BROCCOLI AND NOODLE STIR-FRY

Preparation time: 30 minutes
Servings: 2 to 3

Use a turkey tenderloin and cut it into thin slices across the grain for this dish. Cook the broccoli with the pasta for the last 5 minutes for a shortcut.

4 oz. dried orecchiette or pennette
1 bunch broccoli florets (about 3 cups)
8 oz. turkey tenderloin, cut into thin slices
1 tsp. dry sherry
1 tsp. soy sauce
1 tsp. cornstarch
3 tbs. vegetable oil
4 green onions, thinly sliced

1 quarter-size piece of fresh ginger, peeled and minced
1 small garlic clove, minced
1/2 lb. mushrooms, thinly sliced
1/2 cup chicken broth
1/2 tsp. red pepper flakes
salt and freshly ground pepper
1 tsp. cornstarch dissolved in 1 tbs. soy sauce

Heat pasta water. About 5 minutes before pasta is cooked, add broccoli to cooking water. Combine turkey slices, dry sherry, soy sauce and 1 tsp. cornstarch and let marinate while preparing remaining ingredients. Heat 2 tbs.

vegetable oil in a large nonstick skillet. Sauté onion, ginger and garlic over medium-high heat for 1 minute. Add mushrooms and cook for 2 to 3 minutes. Pour mushrooms out on a plate. Add remaining vegetable oil to skillet and sauté turkey pieces 2 to 3 minutes, stirring constantly. Add chicken broth, red pepper, salt, pepper and mushrooms. Bring to a boil.

Pour hot drained pasta and broccoli into skillet with turkey and toss to combine. Bring sauce a boil and add a small amount of dissolved cornstarch to thicken sauce just enough to coat meat. Serve immediately on warm plates.

TURKEY AND RED PEPPER PASTA

Preparation time: 30 minutes
Servings: 2 to 3

This recipe goes really fast if you have cooked turkey or chicken on hand. Use corkscrew or radiatore pasta to capture the delicious sauce.

6 oz. dried pasta corkscrews or radiatore
1 tbs. butter
½ cup chopped onion
½ lb. mushrooms,
1 medium red pepper, peeled and cut into ¾-inch squares
1½ cups diced cooked turkey
⅓ cup chicken broth
2 tbs. heavy cream
dash red pepper flakes
salt and freshly ground pepper
grated Parmesan cheese
fresh tomato, peeled and chopped for garnish

Bring pasta water to a boil. Cook pasta according to package directions. While water is heating, melt butter in a large nonstick skillet. Sauté onions for 2 to 3 minutes to soften. Over medium high heat, sauté mushrooms 2 to 3 minutes. Add red pepper pieces, turkey, chicken stock, cream, salt, pepper and red pepper flakes. Cook for about 5 minutes until sauce thickens. Turn off heat and set aside until pasta is cooked. Add hot cooked, drained pasta to skillet and toss with sauce to combine. Pour into a warm serving bowl and sprinkle with Parmesan cheese and fresh tomato pieces. Serve immediately on warm plates. Pass additional Parmesan cheese.

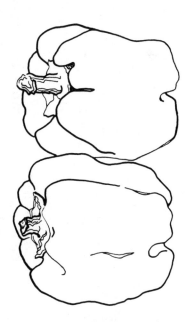

SMOKED TURKEY WITH LINGUINE

Preparation time: 20 minutes
Servings: 2 to 3

Smoked turkey or chicken strips make a rich tasting pasta dish. Add some fresh tomato pieces for color just before serving.

4 oz. dried linguine or 6 oz. fresh
4 oz. smoked turkey, cut into thin
  2-inch x ¼-inch pieces
2 tbs. butter
3 green onions, thinly sliced
2 medium carrots, cut into same
  size strips as turkey

2 tbs. chicken stock or dry white wine
2 tbs. heavy cream
½ tsp. dried tarragon
salt and freshly ground pepper
1 medium tomato, peeled, seeded,
  chopped
grated Parmesan cheese

Bring pasta water to a boil. Heat butter in a medium nonstick skillet. Sauté onions and carrots 3 to 4 minutes until onion softens. Add chicken stock, cream, tarragon, salt and pepper, and simmer 2 to 3 minutes. Pour drained hot pasta into skillet. Add turkey pieces, toss to combine with sauce. Pour into a warm serving bowl, top with tomato pieces, and serve immediately on warm plates. Pass Parmesan cheese.

PASTA WITH SAUSAGE SAUCE

Preparation time: 15 minutes
Cooking time: 30 minutes
Servings: 3 to 4

This is an excellent sauce to make ahead. It goes together very quickly if you use a food processor to chop the onion, green pepper and sausage meat.

12 oz. fresh pasta or 8 oz. dried pasta
4 mild or hot Italian sausages
1 small yellow onion, finely chopped
1 small green pepper, finely chopped
1 can (28 oz.) Italian-style tomatoes

⅓ cup dry red wine
2 tsp. dried oregano
salt and pepper
2 tbs. minced parsley

Have pasta cooking water hot and time pasta to be done when sauce is ready. Remove sausage casings. Flatten sausages to about ⅜-inch thick. Place in a cold skillet, heat and brown on both sides. Remove from pan and pour out all but 2 tbs. of fat. Add onion and green pepper to skillet. Cook over low heat 3 to 4 minutes until softened. While onion and peppers are cooking, drain tomatoes in a sieve over a bowl. Cut out tough stem ends and squeeze out most of the seeds. Coarsely chop tomatoes and sausages. Add tomatoes and their juice, chopped sausages, wine, oregano, salt and pepper to skillet. Simmer, uncovered, 30 minutes. Serve over hot, well-drained pasta on warm plates.

RAVIOLI

Ravioli are little squares or circles of flat pasta filled with meat, cheese, or other good things, and served with a sauce or melted butter and cheese. There are many prepared kinds of ravioli available in the fresh pasta section of most supermarkets. If you want to make your own fillings, consider using won ton wrappers, either folded over the filling in triangle shapes, or using 2 squares with the filling sandwiched between the wrappers.

HOMEMADE RAVIOLI

Making your own pasta for ravioli is a good rainy afternoon project. Start by preparing your filling, and then refrigerate it so that it has a chance to stiffen for easier handling. This step is particularly important if you are using a cheese filling made with ricotta cheese. Then make your pasta dough, using the basic homemade pasta recipe on page 9. Roll out the dough as thinly as possible. Do not let it dry because it becomes difficult to fill and cut. Cover the portion of dough not being used with a damp towel to prevent it from drying out.

Ravioli can be made with a ravioli form which turns out 10 or 12 at a time, or they can be stamped out individually with a single ravioli cutter or round cookie cutter, or they can be made free-form on a large sheet of pasta using a kitchen knife to cut the squares. There is also a slotted or ridged rolling pin which marks the filled ravioli squares for cutting.

If you are using a ravioli form: Cut the dough into strips about 1 inch wider and 1 inch longer than the form. If it is a two-part form, flour the metal frame and place one strip of dough over the top. Place the other half of the form which has small indentations in it, directly on top of the pasta dough. Press down lightly to mark filling depressions, and remove form. Place a small amount of filling, usually ½ to 1 teaspoon depending on size of the ravioli, in each depression. Overfilling may cause the ravioli to break open during cooking. Brush edges of each ravioli with a little water. A pastry brush works well for this. Place another strip of dough over top of filling. Gently press down dough along ridges of the ravioli form. With a heavy rolling pin, roll across ravioli form two or three times to cut dough into individual squares. They will not come completely apart with this rolling. Gently turn ravioli out of the form, flat side down onto a floured cookie sheet. Cover with a towel and let rest an hour before cooking. As the ravioli dry they will break apart easily.

If you are using a single ravioli or cookie cutter: Cut as many squares or circles as possible out of the dough. Place a small amount of filling on half of the squares or circles. Brush edges with a little water. Place another square or circle directly on top of filling and firmly press each ravioli around the edges. Place on a floured cookie sheet or plate, cover with a towel, and let rest an hour before cooking. Ravioli will expand in size during cooking, so if you have a large cutter you may wish to make triangles or half circles from one piece of cut dough rather than using two pieces to form the ravioli.

To make ravioli without a form: Cut a straight line across the top of the dough with a knife or fluted pastry cutter. Place small amounts of filling about 1½ inches apart, 2½ inches down from the cut edge. Brush dough with a little water in a straight line below filling and in between the fillings, making square outlines. Fold down cut edge over filling. Press down firmly along bottom edge of the folded-over pasta dough and then cut out individual ravioli as uniformly as possible. Using a fork, press edges together well to be sure a good seal is formed. Using the bottom line you have just cut for the top of the dough, continue placing filling 1½ inches apart, 2½ inches down from the top edge, and repeat the moistening and cutting process until you have used all the filling. Place ravioli on a floured cookie sheet or plate, cover, and let rest 1 hour before cooking. After ravioli are made, they may be refrigerated prior to cooking.

To cook ravioli: Bring 6 to 8 quarts of water to a rapid boil. Add 1 tbs. salt. Slide in ravioli and cook for 10 to 12 minutes, depending thickness of dough and size. Drain well and pour into a heated bowl. Cover with sauce or melted butter and Parmesan cheese. Serve immediately on warm plates. If desired, cooked ravioli can be added to beef or chicken broth and served as a hearty soup.

Ravioli fillings: Fillings can be made with a wide variety of foods. Chicken, shrimp, clams, veal, sun-dried tomatoes, spinach and cheese used alone or in combinations make good fillings. Cooked meat should be minced or ground and then seasoned and mixed with beaten egg to hold the filling together. Classic ravioli fillings tend to be very lightly seasoned so they are complemented with flavorful tomato sauces or pesto. A little melted butter and some Parmesan cheese is always a welcome finish for freshly cooked ravioli.

Won ton wrappers: We have found the fresh won ton wrappers make excellent quick ravioli. Moisten the edges with a little water before folding or sealing in the filling.

These recipes can be easily doubled if you wish to make more ravioli.

GOAT CHEESE AND SUN-DRIED TOMATO FILLING

Preparation time: 30 minutes
Makes 20

Use fresh wonton wrappers for the ravioli, either folding into triangles or using two wrappers for larger squares. This is a savory filling that only needs a little melted butter and a sprinkle of Parmesan cheese for a sauce. Four or five ravioli make a satisfying first course serving. Make the filling ahead and refrigerate until ready to use.

20-24 fresh won ton wrappers, 3 inches x 3 inches
4 oz. fresh goat cheese
⅓ cup coarsely chopped sun-dried tomatoes
1 egg
generous amounts of freshly ground black pepper
½ tsp. dried oregano
¼ cup grated Parmesan cheese
3 tbs. butter melted in a large skillet

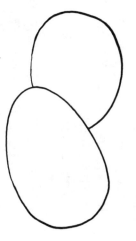

Heat pasta water. Mix goat cheese, sun-dried tomatoes, egg, oregano and Parmesan cheese. If making triangle-shaped ravioli, spread about 1 to 1½ tsp. goat cheese mixture in the center of the won ton wrapper. Brush two adjacent edges with water. Carefully fold the won ton wrapper into a triangle, firmly pressing one unmoistened edge to the moistened edge. Press out as much air as possible and press the remaining edges of the triangle together. Allow to dry for a few minutes on a rack. Continue until all the ravioli are assembled. Use a fluted ravioli cutter for a decorative edge, if desired.

When pasta water is boiling, slip ravioli into water and gently cook 3 to 4 minutes until ravioli float to the top. Remove from water with a flat strainer, drain well, and place in a skillet with melted butter. Over medium heat, turn ravioli in melted butter and pour out on heated plates. Pass additional Parmesan cheese.

BLACK OLIVE PASTE
AND RICOTTA FILLING

Preparation time: 30 minutes
Makes 20 to 22

Here is a zesty, quick ravioli filling. Use fresh wonton wrappers for quick assembly.

20-22 won ton wrappers, 3 inches x 3 inches
4 oz. ricotta
1 egg
2 tbs. black olive paste
¼ cup grated Parmesan cheese
2 tbs. finely chopped Italian parsley
2 tbs. finely chopped fresh sweet basil
3 tbs. butter, melted in a large skillet
grated Parmesan cheese

Heat pasta water to boiling. Combine ricotta, egg, black olive paste, Parmesan cheese, Italian parsley and sweet basil in a small bowl. Using won ton wrappers, place approximately 1 to 1½ tsp. filling in the center of the square. Use closer to 1 tsp. of filling if making triangle shapes. Moisten two adjacent won ton wrapper edges with water. Fold over one unmoistened edge of the triangle to a moistened edge, gently press out as much air as possible and press the remaining edges of the triangle together. Allow to dry on a rack until ready to cook. Cook ravioli in boiling water 3 to 4 minutes until ravioli float to the top. Drain well with a slotted spoon and place in skillet with melted butter over medium low heat. Turn to coat cooked ravioli and serve on warm plates. Pass additional Parmesan cheese.

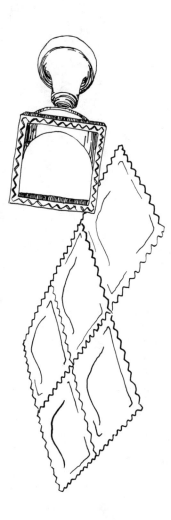

CHEESE FILLING FOR RAVIOLI

Preparation time: 10 minutes
Makes 20 to 24 ravioli

This is a simple, classic cheese filling for ravioli. Mix it up ahead and refrigerate it until you are ready to make the ravioli, or double the recipe if you want to make a larger batch. After cooking, serve with a sauce or gently toss with a little melted butter and some Parmesan cheese.

¾ cup ricotta cheese
½ cup grated Parmesan cheese
2 tbs. minced Italian flat leaf parsley
1 egg

generous amount of white pepper
dash nutmeg
salt
½ tsp. grated lemon rind

Combine all ingredients in a small bowl. Mix until smooth. Refrigerate until ready to fill ravioli. Use about 1½ teaspoons of filling for each ravioli, depending on size.

Follow instructions for filling and cooking won ton wrappers on pages 144-145.

CHICKEN AND SAUSAGE RAVIOLI FILLING

This filling is quickly done in the food processor. Serve with a light tomato sauce, or moisten with a little chicken broth and pass extra Parmesan cheese.

3 tbs. parsley, stems removed
1 cup diced cooked chicken
1 mild or hot Italian sausage, cooked, crumbled

1 egg
salt and freshly ground pepper
½ tsp. Worcestershire sauce
¼ cup grated Parmesan cheese

Chop parsley in a food processor, add cooked chicken and sausage, and process until mixture is minced. Add remaining ingredients and process for another minute until ingredients are well combined. Refrigerate filling until ready to use. Follow instructions for filling won ton wrappers on pages 144-145. If using won ton wrappers, cook in a large amount of hot boiling water for 3 to 4 minutes. Homemade pasta squares take approximately 10 to 12 minutes to cook.

BAKED PASTA DISHES

Lasagne is taking on a new look with vegetables replacing the traditional meat and tomato sauce. New no-cook or instant lasagne noodles are available and produce a tender, delicate pasta layer. These noodles can be soaked in hot water for 4 to 5 minutes and cut to form wrappers for ravioli or cannelloni. Egg roll wrappers, about 6 inches square, also can be used for fresh pasta in lasagne or cannelloni dishes if you cook them in boiling water for about 2 minutes before using them. Some pasta shops sell fresh wide lasagne noodles by the pound if you don't want to take the time to make your own.

Included in this section are some new favorite lasagne recipes. There is a zesty *Swiss Chard and Black Olive* combination, and a fresh *Red Pepper and Ham Lasagne*. Shrimp and scallops are folded into a lemony tarragon sauce and layered with tender no-boil noodles for an elegant *Seafood Lasagne*. Asparagus and goat cheese are used to fill cannelloni made with the instant lasagne noodles. There are other baked dishes, too — *Walnut Chicken and Noodle Casserole*, and a good *Armenian Pilaf*. We also include our longtime favorite cannelloni, which makes great party fare.

SWISS CHARD AND BLACK OLIVE LASAGNE

Preparation time: 45 minutes
Baking time: 25 minutes
Servings: 3 to 4

No-boil or instant type lasagne noodles are layered with a robust filling of Swiss chard, ricotta, peppers and black olive paste. Cover the instant lasagne noodles with hot water for 4 to 5 minutes to soften them before using in recipe.

1 recipe *Bechamel Sauce*, page 153
1 bunch red or green Swiss chard, approximately 1 lb.
2 tbs. full-flavored olive oil
1 large onion, chopped
2 garlic cloves, minced
1 red or orange pepper, peeled, diced
lasagne noodles, instant type softened in hot water, or fresh egg roll wrappers, or regular lasagne noodles, cooked according to package directions

1 egg
4 oz. ricotta
3 tbs. black olive paste
½ tsp. dried thyme or 1 tbs. fresh thyme
generous amounts of freshly ground black pepper
grated Parmesan cheese for topping

Make *Bechamel Sauce* and set aside. Prepare Swiss chard by stripping leaves from stems and discarding stems. Chop leaves into 1-inch or smaller pieces.

There will be about 4 cups. Heat olive oil in a large skillet. Add onion and sauté 6 to 8 minutes until onion softens. Add chard, garlic and red pepper. Continue to cook until all liquid has evaporated and chard has softened. Allow mixture to cool before adding to ricotta mixture.

If using instant lasagne noodles, soften 4 large or 8 small pieces to make 4 layers in hot water 3 to 4 minutes before using. If using traditional dried lasagne, cook according to package directions.

Beat egg lightly in a large mixing bowl. Whisk in ricotta, thyme, black olive paste and generous amounts of black pepper. Combine cooled chard mixture with ricotta and ½ cup of *Bechamel Sauce*. Preheat oven to 350°.

To assemble: Reserve 1 cup of *Bechamel Sauce* for the top layer. Spread a thin layer of sauce in the bottom of an 8-inch-square baking pan. Top with 1 lasagne layer. Spread with about ⅓ of chard mixture and about ⅓ of the remaining sauce. Continue with another lasagne layer, chard and sauce, making 2 more layers. Finish with the last lasagne layer and spread with reserved cup of sauce. Sprinkle with Parmesan cheese. Cover with foil and bake in a preheated 350° oven for 15 minutes. Uncover, bake for another 10 minutes, and run under the broiler to lightly brown the top. Allow to rest 5 minutes before serving. If assembling in advance and refrigerating, add an additional 15 minutes baking time.

RED PEPPER AND HAM LASAGNE

Preparation time: 45 minutes
Baking time: 25 minutes
Servings: 4 to 5

Try the instant or no-boil lasagne noodles to save some time. Cover the noodles with hot water for 4 to 5 minutes to soften before layering in the pan. These noodles are much thinner than the regular lasagne strips; if you use traditional dried lasagne noodles you may wish to make fewer layers. The crisp red peppers and slivered ham slices add a nice texture to the finished dish.

Bechamel Sauce, page 153
1 cup red onion, chopped
3 tbs. olive oil
1 lb. mushrooms, sliced
2 garlic cloves, minced
salt and freshly ground pepper
½ cup slivered ham (4 oz.)
2 medium red, yellow or green
  peppers, peeled, julienned

4 tbs. minced Italian parsley
grated Parmesan cheese
  for topping
lasagne noodles, instant type
  softened in hot water, or fresh egg
  roll wrappers, or regular lasagne
  noodles, cooked according to
  package directions

Make *Bechamel Sauce* and set aside. Heat olive oil in a large skillet. Sauté onions in olive oil for 3 to 4 minutes until onions soften. Turn up heat and add mushrooms. Sauté for 3 to 4 minutes until mushrooms release moisture. Add garlic and cook for 1 to 2 minutes. When mushrooms have softened, turn off heat and set aside. Tilt pan so juices collect and add juices to *Bechamel Sauce*. Preheat oven to 350°.

To assemble: Spoon a thin layer of *Bechamel Sauce* on bottom of a lasagne baking dish (8-inch square pan). Top with a layer of lasagne. Add another thin layer of sauce, top with a single layer of julienned peppers, some sautéed mushrooms and another lasagne layer. Top with more sauce, some slivered ham, mushrooms, parsley, and peppers. Continue to layer, using 5 to 6 lasagne layers. Top last lasagne layer with sauce and sprinkle with additional Parmesan cheese. Bake at 350° for about 20 to 25 minutes, or until lasagne is very hot. Run under the broiler for 1 to 2 minutes to lightly brown the top. Let stand 5 minutes before serving.

Bechamel Sauce

4 tbs. butter
3 tbs. flour
2 cups milk

salt and freshly ground pepper
½ cup Parmesan cheese
dash nutmeg

Melt butter in a small saucepan. Stir in flour and cook over low heat for 3 minutes. Gradually add milk. Cook until sauce thickens. Stir in remaining ingredients. Cook 3 to 4 minutes.

SEAFOOD LASAGNE

Preparation time: 30 minutes
Baking time: 20 minutes
Servings: 3 to 4

Small bay scallops and shrimp folded into a creamy tarragon sauce are baked between tender lasagne noodles for an elegant first course or luncheon dish. Try the delicate no-boil or instant lasagne noodles, egg roll wrappers (cooked for 2 minutes), or thin, fresh homemade pasta as the traditional ruffled edged lasagna noodles are too thick for this preparation. Serve with a crisp chardonnay or Pinot Grigio wine.

lasagne noodles, instant type softened in hot water, or fresh egg roll wrappers, or regular lasagne noodles, cooked according to package directions
3 tbs. butter
2 tbs. shallots, finely chopped
3 tbs. flour
1 cup clam juice
1½ cups light cream
1 tsp. Dijon mustard

2 tbs. lemon juice
½ tsp. dried tarragon
salt and generous amount of white pepper
½ lb. fresh small bay scallops, uncooked
½ lb. small peeled, deveined shrimp, uncooked
⅓ cup grated mozzarella or Parmesan cheese

Preheat oven to 350°. Prepare scallops by removing small white muscle and rinsing well to remove any sand. Peel and devein shrimp. Cut small shrimp in half lengthwise. If using larger shrimp, cut into same size pieces as scallops. Make sauce: Melt butter in a small saucepan. Sauté shallots 1 to 2 minutes to soften. Add flour and cook 1 to 2 minutes. Whisk in clam juice and cream, bring to a boil and cook until sauce thickens. Stir in mustard, lemon juice, tarragon, salt and white pepper. Reserve ¾ cup of sauce for topping. Cover bottom of 8-inch x 8-inch baking pan with a thin layer of sauce. Fold uncooked seafood into remaining hot sauce.

To assemble: Place one lasagne layer on top of sauce in pan. Top with about ¼ of seafood mixture. Continue layering lasagne squares and sauce to make 3 more layers. Top with last lasagne piece. Spread with reserved sauce and sprinkle with grated cheese. Cover with foil and bake in preheated oven for 20 minutes until heated through. Run under the broiler for 1 to 2 minutes to lightly brown top. Allow to stand 5 minutes before serving. There will be extra sauce in the bottom of the baking pan to spoon over the served portions.

ASPARAGUS AND GOAT CHEESE CANNELLONI

Preparation time: 30 minutes
Baking time: 20 minutes
Makes 10 cannelloni

Instant lasagne noodles are stuffed with a savory goat cheese filling and green asparagus tips and baked with a creamy dill sauce. Soften the pasta by soaking in hot water for 3 to 4 minutes, and then cut into approximate squares. If you have thick asparagus, use one per cannelloni.

10 thick or 20 thin asparagus tips
10 cut pasta wrappers, about
3½-inches square

Filling, follows
Sauce, page 157

Filling

4 oz. goat cheese
1 egg
½ tsp. Dijon mustard

1 tbs. minced shallots
1 tbs. lemon juice
2 tbs. grated Parmesan cheese

Microwave shallots with lemon juice about 1 minute on high power. Let cool. Combine remaining filling ingredients; beat until smooth and creamy. Add cooled shallot mixture to filling.

Sauce

2 tbs. butter
2 tbs. flour
1½ cups milk
½ tsp. Worcestershire sauce
1 tbs. finely chopped fresh dill or
1 tsp. dried dillweed
salt and freshly ground pepper
¾ cup grated Gruyére cheese

Melt butter in a small saucepan, add the flour and cook 2 minutes. Gradually add milk, stirring to make a smooth sauce. Cook over medium heat until sauce thickens and comes to a boil. Add Worcestershire, dill, salt, pepper and half of the Gruyére cheese. Remove from heat and allow to cool slightly before using.

Cut tough ends off asparagus spears. The asparagus should be just a little longer than the pasta squares. Cook asparagus in boiling water for about 5 minutes, drain, and cover with cold water to stop the cooking process.

To assemble: Spread a thin layer of sauce in the bottom of an 8-inch-square baking pan. Spread a pasta square with a thin layer of filling, spreading to edges. Place 2 asparagus spears at one end of pasta and roll up. Place seam side down over sauce in baking pan. Continue to make remaining cannelloni. Top with remaining cheese sauce. Sprinkle with the remaining grated Gruyére. Cover with foil and bake at 350° for 20 minutes until cannelloni are bubbling hot. Uncover and run under the broiler to lightly brown the top.

ORZO AND GREEN CHILE CASSEROLE

Preparation time: 15 minutes
Baking time: 20 minutes
Servings: 4 to 6

Cook the orzo and then fold in diced green chiles, cheese and sour cream and bake. This makes a delicious side dish for a barbecue or a potluck.

½ cups orzo, riso, or other small grain-shaped pasta
½ cup sour cream
½ cup grated sharp cheddar cheese
½ cup canned diced green chiles
2 small tomatoes, peeled, seeded chopped

Cook pasta according to package directions. Drain and pour into an oven-proof baking dish. Stir in sour cream and grated cheese. Fold chiles and tomatoes into pasta and top with Parmesan cheese. Bake at 375° for 20 to 25 minutes until lightly browned and bubbling.

Variation: Substitute 4 oz. goat cheese and ⅓ cup diced sun-dried tomatoes for the cheddar cheese and green chiles.

CANNELLONI

Preparation time: 1 hour
Baking time: 35 minutes
Servings: 6

Fresh homemade pasta squares (see basic recipe, page 9) make the best cannelloni, but packaged manicotti tubes can be used if desired.

Chicken and Mushroom Filling, page 160   18 fresh pasta squares, page 9,
Tomato Sauce, page 161   or softened no-boil lasagne noodles
Cheese Sauce, page 161

If desired, filling and sauces can be made ahead and refrigerated. When ready to use, warm sauces over low heat. Make pasta squares and cook immediately after cutting to prevent their drying out. Cook in rapidly boiling water about 8 minutes. Remove from water and cover with wet paper towels.

To assemble cannelloni: Place 2 to 3 tbs. of filling on the bottom third of each square. Roll into a cylinder. Place rolls seam side down in 1 large or 2 smaller well-buttered baking dishes. Spoon tomato sauce over rolls and top with cheese sauce. Bake at 350° 20 minutes until hot and bubbly.

Cannelloni can be frozen before baking. Allow to defrost in refrigerator. Bake 35 to 40 minutes at 350°. Cover with foil the first 20 minutes.

Wine suggestion: Pinot Noir

Chicken and Mushroom Filling

4 to 5 tbs. olive oil
2 to 2½ lbs. chicken thighs
1 large onion, finely chopped
2 carrots, finely chopped
1 garlic clove, minced
1 cup white wine
½ lb. fresh mushrooms
½ cup finely chopped parsley
1 egg
1 tsp. salt
½ tsp. pepper
½ cup grated Parmesan cheese

Remove skin from chicken. Heat 2 to 3 tablespoons oil in a large skillet. Brown chicken on both sides. Remove from pan. Add onion, carrot and garlic to remaining oil in skillet. Sauté until onion is soft. Scrape up brown bits from bottom of skillet. Return chicken pieces to skillet. Add wine and bring to a boil. Reduce heat and simmer, covered, 45 minutes. Remove from heat. When cool enough to handle, remove chicken from bones. Heat remaining oil in another skillet. Sauté mushrooms 4 to 5 minutes. Add mushrooms to chicken and chop finely in a food processor. Combine mixture with parsley, egg, salt, pepper and Parmesan cheese.

Tomato Sauce

1 tbs. olive oil
1/2 cup chopped onion
1 can (14 oz.) beef broth
1 can (14 oz.) tomato puree

1/4 cup Madeira or Marsala
1/2 tsp. oregano
1 tsp. dried sweet basil
1/2 tsp. sugar

Sauté onion in olive oil until soft. Add remaining ingredients. Bring to a boil. Cook uncovered over medium heat 20 to 25 minutes until sauce reduces and thickens.

Cheese Sauce

3 tbs. butter
3 tbs. flour
2 cups milk
1/2 cup grated Parmesan cheese

salt
1/4 tsp. white pepper
dash nutmeg

Melt butter in a small saucepan. Stir in flour and cook 3 minutes. Gradually add milk. Cook until sauce thickens. Stir in remaining ingredients. Cook 3 to 4 minutes.

VEGETABLE LASAGNE

This dish can be made a day in advance and reheated when needed.

Preparation time: 1 hour
Baking time: 25 minutes
Servings: 4 to 5

Tomato Sauce, page 163
Vegetable Sauce, page 163
lasagne noodles for 4 layers

2 cups ricotta cheese
1/2 cup grated Parmesan cheese

Prepare *Tomato Sauce* and *Vegetable Sauce.* Cook lasagne noodles as directed. Rinse with cold water and drain well. Place one layer of cooked noodles in a buttered 9-x-13-inch baking dish. Top with 1/2 of the vegetable sauce. Spread 1/2 cup ricotta cheese over vegetable layer. Top with another layer of noodles. Repeat vegetable and ricotta cheese layers. Pour about 1/3 cup tomato sauce over ricotta. Top with final layer of lasagne noodles. Spread with remaining ricotta cheese. Distribute remaining tomato sauce over cheese and top with Parmesan cheese. Bake in a 350° oven 20 to 25 minutes until hot and bubbly. If lasagne is frozen, allow to defrost. Cover with foil and heat in a 350° oven 30 minutes. Uncover and bake 10 minutes longer or until thoroughly heated and bubbly. Let stand about 10 minutes before cutting into serving pieces.

Wine suggestion: Zinfandel or Charbono

Tomato Sauce

1 can (15 oz.) tomato puree
1 tsp. dried sweet basil
1 tsp. dried oregano
2 tbs. dry white wine or dry vermouth

Combine tomato puree, basil, oregano and white wine in a small saucepan. Bring to a boil and simmer uncovered over medium heat 10 minutes.

Vegetable Sauce

1/3 cup olive oil
1 cup finely chopped onions
1/4 to 1/2 tsp. hot red pepper flakes
1 lb. fresh mushrooms, coarsely chopped
2 garlic cloves, minced
2 cups coarsely grated carrots
1 green pepper, finely chopped
1 red pepper, finely chopped
1 1/2 cups peeled, diced eggplant
salt and pepper

Heat olive oil in a large skillet. Add onions and pepper flakes; sauté 5 to 6 minutes until onions are soft but not browned. Increase heat. Add mushrooms and sauté 3 to 4 minutes. Add garlic, carrots, peppers, eggplant, salt and pepper. Sauté 3 to 4 minutes. Cover pan and cook over low heat about 15 minutes.

ARMENIAN PILAF

This classic pilaf goes perfectly with lamb shish kebob.

Preparation time: 15 minutes
Baking time: 30 minutes
Servings: 4 to 6

3 cans (14 oz. each) chicken broth
8 tbs. butter (1 cube)

½ cup crushed fine egg noodles
2 cups uncooked long grain rice

Bring chicken broth to a boil in a saucepan. Melt 4 tbs. butter in a 3-quart flameproof casserole with a tightly fitting lid. Add crushed noodles to melted butter and stir until golden brown. Add boiling broth and rice. Stir gently. Boil 5 minutes. Cover casserole and place in a 350° oven 20 to 25 minutes, or until all liquid is absorbed. Stir gently and dot with remaining butter. Return to oven and bake uncovered for 5 minutes. Serve immediately.

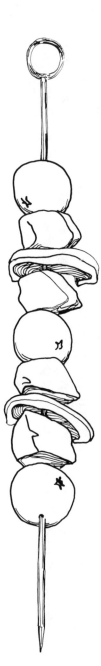

WALNUT CHICKEN AND NOODLE CASSEROLE

Preparation time: 30 minutes
Baking time: 20 to 25 minutes
Servings: 4 to 6

Crunchy walnuts add an interesting texture to this creamy chicken and noodle casserole. Make this with leftover roast chicken or turkey.

12 oz. fresh or 8 oz. dried wide
   noodles or linguine
7 tbs. butter
5 tbs. flour
3 cups chicken broth
1/3 cup dry sherry or white wine
1/2 tsp. paprika

salt and pepper
8 oz. fresh mushrooms, sliced
2-2 1/2 cups diced cooked chicken or
   turkey
1/2 cup coarsley chopped walnuts
grated Parmesan cheese

Cook pasta. Drain well and place in a large buttered casserole. Melt 5 tbs. butter in a saucepan. Add flour. Cook, stirring, 2 minutes. Gradually add chicken broth, sherry, paprika, salt and pepper. Cook, stirring constantly, until sauce thickens. Melt remaining butter in a medium skillet. Sauté mushrooms 4 to 5 minutes. Combine mushrooms, chicken and walnuts with pasta in casserole. Add sauce. Mix carefully and top with Parmesan cheese. Bake at 350° for 20 to 25 minutes until hot and bubbly.

Wine suggestion: Chardonnay, Sauvignon Blanc or Dry Riesling

COMMERCIAL PASTA SHAPES: A GLOSSARY

agnolotti - Round ravioli, usually stuffed with a meat filling.

anellini - Little rings. Can be baked in sauce or added to soups.

angel hair - "Capelli D'Angelo." Long, very thin strands. Because of their delicacy best served with light sauces.

bucatini - Hollow long pasta tubes, a little thicker than spaghetti.

cannelloni - Squares of sheet pasta, stuffed, rolled into cylinders, sauced and baked.

cappelletti - Called "little hats" because of their cap shape.

conchiglie - Also called "sea shells." Fluted shell-shaped pasta either ridged or smooth. The larger sizes can be stuffed and baked.

farfalle - Butterfly or bow tie shaped pasta, available in many sizes.

fettuccine - Ribbon noodles about ¼-inch wide, served with a wide variety of sauces, the most familiar being Fettuccine Alfredo.

fusilli - Spiral shaped spaghetti strands.

gemellini - Hollow tubes twisted around each other and cut into 1½-inch lengths.

gnocchi - A small dumpling made of potatoes, flour or semolina. Sometimes spinach or other flavorings are added. Usually boiled and served with butter and cheese.

lasagne - A wide flat noodle baked in layers with meat or vegetable filling.

linguine - A ribbon noodle narrower than fettuccine.

macaroni - This is the Italian word for all pasta. The common usage means pasta tubes, which can be short, long, thick, thin, curved or straight.

manicotti - Either a large 4-inch long, 1-inch diameter tube, or a square of flat pasta which is stuffed, rolled into a cylinder, sauced and baked.

mostaccioli - Almost identical to penne.

noodles - Thin ribbons of flat pasta, often containing eggs, available in widths from ⅛-inch to over 1 inch.

orecchiette - Small ear-shaped pieces of pasta.

pansoti - A stuffed dumpling similar to ravioli, usually triangular in shape.

pappardelle - Very thin 1-inch or wider strips of pasta. Often served with ragout of game.

penne - Tubular pasta with ends cut at an angle. Good with rich sauces or in baked dishes.

ravioli - A well known square pasta dumpling stuffed with various meat, cheese or vegetable fillings.

radiatore - "Little radiators." A newer shape, compact with numerous ridges to hold sauce. Dense and compact. Does well with hearty sauces.

rigatoni - Hollow macaroni tubes about ½-inch in diameter by 2 inches long.

rotelle - Small wagon wheel shaped pasta.

spaghetti - Thin, solid round pasta strings, any length.

spirali - Corkscrew shaped pasta. Pretty in salads.

tagliatelle - Flat egg noodles,ranging from ½-inch to ⅝-inch wide.

tortellini - Small ring or half moon-shaped stuffed pasta. Available both dried and fresh.

tubetti - Short tubular pasta, also known as salad macaroni.

ziti - Smaller and smoother type of rigatoni, about ½-inch thick.

INDEX